Juliusz Slowacki's Agamemnon's Tomb

Other Books of Interest from St. Augustine's Press

Zbigniew Janowski, *Augustinian-Cartesian Index*

Zbigniew Janowski, *How to Read Descartes's* Meditations

Leszek Kolakowski, *The Two Eyes of Spinoza*

Leszek Kolakowski, *My Correct Views on Everything*

Leszek Kolakowski, *Husserl and the Search for Certitude*

Leszek Kolakowksi, *Religion If There Is No God...*

Leszek Kolakowski, *Bergson*

Emanuela Scribano, *A Reading Guide to Descartes'*
Meditations on First Philosophy

Roger Kimball, *The Fortunes of Permanence*

Richard A. Watson, *The Philosopher's Enigma*

Jean-Luc Marion, *Descartes's Grey Ontology*

Richard A. Watson, *Descartes's Ballet*

Étienne Gilson, *Theology and the Cartesian Doctrine of Freedom*

La Rochefoucauld, *Maxims*

Percy Bysshe Shelley (translator), *The Symposium of Plato*

John Deely, *Semiotic Animal*

Denise Schaeffer (editor), *Writing the Poetic Soul of Philosophy:*
Essays in Honor of Michael Davis

Joseph Pearce, *Death Comes for the War Poets: A Verse Tapestry*

Josef Pieper, *Enthusiasm and Divine Madness*

Josef Pieper, *Don't Worry about Socrates*

Seth Benardete, *Achilles and Hector: The Homeric Hero*

Peter Kreeft, *If Einstein Had Been a Surfer*

Roger Scruton, *Perictione in Colophon*

Juliusz Slowacki's
Agamemnon's Tomb

A Polish Oresteia

Catherine O'Neil and Zbigniew Janowski

ST. AUGUSTINE'S PRESS
South Bend, Indiana

Manufactured in the United States of America.

1 2 3 4 5 6   25 24 23 22 21 20 19

Library of Congress Cataloging in Publication Data
O'Neil, Catherine, 1964-
Juliusz Slowacki's Agamemnon's tomb : a Polish oresteia /
Catherine O'Neil with Zbigniew Janowski;
translation by Catherine O'Neil.
p. cm.
Includes bibliographical references and index.
ISBN 978-1-58731-017-1 (pbk.)
1. Slowacki, Juliusz, 1809-1849--Criticism and interpretation.
2. Slowacki, Juliusz, 1809-1849. Grsb Agamemnona. 3. Polish
poetry--19th century--Translations into English. 4. Polish poetry--
Classical influences. 5. Polish poetry--Themes, motives. 6. Roman-
ticism--Europe. I. Janowski, Zbigniew. II. Slowacki, Juliusz,
1809-1849. Grsb Agamemnona. III. Title. IV. Title: Agamemnon's
tomb.
PG7158.S6Z83 2011
891.8'516--dc23
2011039531

St. Augustine's Press
www.staugustine.net

For our daughter Krista ("Kid")
and
in memory of a dear friend,
Hanna Olewicz-Legutko

Table of Contents

Preface

Juliusz Słowacki's *Agamemnon's Tomb* is many things in Polish literary history. But first and foremost it is read as an elaborate castigation of the Polish people, accusing them as it does of the vices of slavishness and imitation nearly ten years after the failed uprising against Russia in November 1830. Its last line, at least in the version that has been canonical for over one hundred and seventy years, declares to Poland: "For you have no power to curse – you slave." As Czesław Miłosz remarks, "Some lines that have become proverbial show Słowacki's typical aggressiveness in his attitude toward his country."[1]

Written in 1836, *Agamemnon's Tomb* was published only in 1840 as a kind of epilogue to Słowacki's historical drama *Lilla Weneda*. Out of the 32 stanzas in the manuscript text, Słowacki's published version included only 21. (The line quoted above is its "last" word.) The remaining stanzas were published by later editors as Canto 8 of his travelogue, *Voyage to the Holy Land from Naples*. With the exception of a handful of Słowacki scholars, the poem resonates in Polish ears as an angry didactic addressed by Słowacki to his fellow countrymen.

---

1 Czesław Miłosz, *A History of Polish Literature* (Berkeley: University of California Press, 1983), p. 238.

Be that as it may, the poem's reception in Poland is one thing, but its universal value, worthy of interest among non-Polish readers, is another. It is the latter that the present work attempts to bring forth: Słowacki as a European Romantic, well established in the same heritage that was the well of inspiration for Goethe, Byron, Shelley or Keats. As we have tried to show in our commentary to the poem, the universal appeal of *Agamemnon's Tomb* lies in Słowacki's ingenious use of Greek dramatic heritage.

"We are all Greeks," Shelley wrote once, pointing to Europe's cultural debt to Greece. In *Agamemnon's Tomb*, Słowacki expressed the same thing: the Polish experience can be read through the prism of a "universal" Greek experience and Poland's achievements and failures can be measured against the Greek standard.

The last decade or so has brought many valuable studies in Polish on Słowacki and Greek Antiquity which put *Agamemnon's Tomb* in its proper perspective. The Greek tragedies were also the inspiration for the Greek structure of his *Lilla Weneda*, the play Słowacki originally published with *Agamemnon's Tomb*. Read through the "prism" of Greeks tragedies, *Agamemnon's Tomb* is a poetic Polish Oresteia: a story of "fame, crime, and pride" (stanza 5). In the poem we find all the characters – Agamemnon, Electra, Clytemnestra, made to speak by Słowacki in the language of the Greek playwrights.

The present translation of *Agamemnon's Tomb* is not the first one in the English language but is the first complete one. There are two other translations of stanzas 1–21: by M.A. Michael published in 1944 in England (included in *Polish Anthology*, ed. by Tadeusz M. Filip, Duckworth, 1944), and by Michael J. Mikoś in his volume of translations of Słowacki's poetry, *This Fateful Power. Sesquicentennial Anthology 1809–1849* (Lublin: Norbertinum, 1999).

Literature on Słowacki in English is hardly existent and the translations of his works are a rarity. With the exception of the small anthology by Mikoś mentioned above and the recent Cambridge Scholars edition *Poland's Angry Romantic* (Cambridge: Cambridge Scholars, 2009), which includes the present translation of *Agamemnon's Tomb* and two major works, *Balladina* and *Beniowski*, there are no substantial works by Słowacki available in English or works on him. The present work will hopefully fill in a gap in the knowledge of Słowacki in the English-speaking world. It is also the first in any language that offers an overarching analysis of the entire poem. As such it contains all the shortcomings of a pioneer work and we can only hope for patience on the part of our critics.

We would like to thank professors Maria Kalinowska (University of Nicolas Copernicus, Poland) and Andrzej Waśko (Jagiellonian University, Poland) for reading the manuscript and for their suggestions. Without their works on Polish Romanticism and friendly comments this text would be much less than it is. We would also like to express gratitude to Professor Kalinowska for making available to us Słowacki's manuscript of her forthcoming critical edition of the *Voyage to the Holy Land*. Finally, we would like to thank Cambridge Scholars for kind permission to reproduce here our translation of *Agamemnon's Tomb* which first appeared in *Poland's Angry Romantic*.

Catherine O'Neil and Zbigniew Janowski
Christmas 2018

Grób Agamemnona

[1]
Niech fantastycznie lutnia nastrojona
Wtóruje myśli posępnej i ciemnej,
Bom oto wstąpił w gròb Agamemnona
I siedzę cichy w kopule podziemnej,
Co krwią Atrydów zwalana okrutną.
Serce zasnęło, lecz śni. Jak mi smutno!

[2]
O! jak daleko brzmi ta harfa złota,
Ktòrej mi tylko echo wiecznie słychać!
Druidyczna to z głazów wielkich grota,
Gdzie wiatr przychodzi po szczelinach wzdychać
I ma Elektry głos – ta bieli płòtno
I odzywa się z laurów: "Jak mi smutno!"

[3]
Tu po kamieniach z pracowną Arachną
Kłòci się wietrzyk i rwie jej przędziwo,
Tu cząbry smutne gòr spalonych pachną,
Tu wiatr, obiegłszy gòrę ruin siwą,
Napędza nasion kwiatów – a te puchy
Chodzą i w grobie latają jak duchy,

[4]
Tu świerszcze polne, pomiędzy kamienie
Przed nagrobowym pochowane słońcem,
Jakby mi chciały nakazać milczenie,
Sykają. Strasznym jest rapsodu końcem
Owe sykanie, co się w grobach słyszy –
Jest objawieniem, hymnem, pieśnią ciszy.

Agamemnon's Tomb

[1]
Let my magically strung lute
Resound more gloomily and more darkly,
For I have entered Agamemnon's tomb,
And I sit quietly in the underground dome
Caked in the blood of the cruel Atreides.
My heart is asleep, but still it dreams. How sad I am!

[2]
O! How far off sounds that golden harp,
Whose eternal echo is all that I hear!
This is a druidic grotto of great stones,
Where the wind comes in to sigh in the cracks
And brings me Electra's voice: she whitens the wash
And calls from the laurel trees: "How sad I am!"

[3]
Here among the stones busy Arachne
Quarrels with the breeze, which tears her yarn.
Here the fragrance of sad savory drifts over scorched
mountains,
Here the wind, whipping through the grey piles of ruins,
Drives flower seeds on – and the down
Wanders and flits around the tomb like spirits.

[4]
Here field crickets among the stones,
Hiding from the sun that shines above the tomb,
Hiss as if they wished to silence me.
This hissing that one hears in tombs
Is a terrifying coda to a song –
A revelation, a hymn, a song of silence.

[5]
O! cichy jestem jak wy, o Atrydzi!
Których popioły śpią pod świerszczòw strażą.
Ani mię teraz moja małość wstydzi,
Ani się myśli tak jak orły ważą.
Głęboko jestem pokorny i cichy
Tu, w tym grobowcu sławy, zbrodni, pychy.

[6]
Nad drzwiami grobu, na granitu zrębie
Wyrasta dąbek w tròjkącie z kamieni;
Posadziły go wròble lub gołębie
I listkami się czerni zieleni,
I słońca w ciemny grobowiec nie puszcza;
Zerwałem jeden liść z czarnego kuszcza;

[7]
Nie bronił mi go żaden duch ni mara,
Ani w gałązkach jęknłęo widziadło,
Tylko sie słońcu stała większa szpara
I wbiegło złote, i do nóg mi padło.
Zrazu myślałem, że ten, co się wdziera,
Blask – była struna to z harfy Homera;

[8]
I wyciągnąłem rękę na ciemności,
By ją ułowić i napiąć, i drżącą
Przymusić do łez i śpiewu, i złości
Nad wielkim niczym grobòw i milczącą
Garstka popiołów – ale w moim ręku
Ta struna drgnęła i pękła bez jęku

[9]
Tak więc – to los moj na grobowcach siadać

[5]
I am quiet like you, o Atreides!
Whose ashes sleep beneath the watchful crickets.
Neither am I ashamed of my insignificance
Nor do my thoughts soar like eagles.
I am deeply humble and calm here,
In this tomb of fame, crime, pride.

[6]
A young oak shoots up in the stone triangle
On the carved granite over the door to the tomb.
It was planted by sparrows, or maybe pigeons,
And blooms black leaves that do not allow
The sun to enter the dark tomb;
I plucked one leaf from the black bush;

[7]
No spirit or ghost wrested it from me,
Nor did a specter groan in the branches;
Only the shaft of sunlight grew bigger,
And golden light spilled at my feet.
I thought at once that this brightness breaking in
Was a string from Homer's harp;

[8]
And I stretched my hand out in the darkness,
To tune it and pluck it and, trembling,
Force it to tears and to song – and to anger
At the great nothingness of graves and this silent
Handful of dust. But in my hand
This string trembled and vanished without complaint.

[9]
And so – it is my fate to sit on tombstones

I szukać smutkow błachych, wiotkich, kruchych.
To los mój senne królestwa posiadać,
Nieme mieć harfy i słuchaczów głóchych
Albo umarłych – i tak pełen wstrętu . . .
Na koń! Chcę słońca, wichru i tętentu!

[10]
No koń!... Tu łożem suchego potoku,
Gdzie zamiast wody płynie laur ròżowy,
Ze łzą i z wielką błyskawicą w oku,
Jakby mie wicher gnał błyskawicowy,
Lecę, a koń się na powietrzu kładnie;
Jeśli napotka grób rycerzy – padnie.

[11]
Na Termopilach? Nie, na Cheronei
Trzeba się memu załamać koniowi,
Bo jestem z kraju, gdzie widmo nadziei
Dla małowiernych serc podobne snowi.
Wiec jeśli koń mòj w biegu się przestraszy,
To tej mogiły, co równa jest – naszéj.

[12]
Mnie od mogiły termopilskiej gotów
Odgonić legion umarłych Spartanów,
Bo jestem z kraju smutnego ilotów,
Z kraju – gdzie rozpacz nie sypie kurchanów,
Z kraju – gdzie zawsze po dniach nieszczęsliwych
Zostaje smutne pół – rycerzy – żywych.

[13]
Na Termopliach ja się nie odważę
Osadzić konia w wąwozowym szlaku;
Bo tam być muszą tak patrzące twarze,

And seek out insignificant, frail sorrows.
It is my fate to rule over sleepy kingdoms,
To have mute harps and deaf listeners.
Or dead ones. And so, full of disgust . . .
To horse! I want sun, wind, the sound of hoof beats!

[10]
To horse!... Here, along the bed of a dry stream,
Where pink laurel blossoms flow instead of water,
As if a shining storm were chasing me,
I fly with tears and with intense, flashing eyes,
And my horse's legs stretch out on the wind.
If he stumbles over a grave where knights rest – he'll fall.

[11]
At Thermopylae? – No, at Chaeronea –
That is where my horse must stop.
For I am from a land where the specter of hope
Is like a dream for hearts of little faith.
For if my horse is frightened in his flight,
Then that grave is equal to – ours.

[12]
A legion of dead Spartans is ready
To chase me from the grave at Thermopylae,
For I am from the sad land of Ilots,
From a land where despair does not rain down on graves,
From a land where always after unhappy days
There remains a sad half of knights – alive.

[13]
At Thermopylae I will not dare
To lead my horse through the pass;
For there must be such faces there, whose gaze

Że serce skruszy wstyd – w każdym Polaku.
Ja tam nie będę stał przed Grecji duchem –
Nie – pierwej skonam, niż tam iść – z łańcuchem.

[14]
Na Termopilach – jaką bym zdał sprawę,
Gdyby stanęli męże nad mogiłą
I pokazawszy mi swe piersi krwawe
Potem spytali wręcz: "W i e l e w a s b y ł o?
Zapomnij, że jest długi wieków przedział."
Gdyby spytali tak – coż bym powiedział?

[15]
Na Termopilach, bez złotego pasa,
Bez czerwonego leży trup kontusza,
Ale jest nagi trup Leonidasa,
Jest w marmurowych kształtach piękna dusza;
I długo płakał lud takiej ofiary,
Ognia wonnego i rozbitej czary.

[16]
O Polsko! Póki ty duszę anielską
Będziesz więziła w czerepie rubasznym,
Póty kat będzie rąbał twoje cielsko,
Póty nie będzie twòj miecz zemsty strasznym,
Póty mieć będziesz hyjenę na sobie
I gròb – i oczy otworzone w grobie!

[17]
Zrzuć do ostatka te płachty ohydne,
Te – Dejaniry palącą koszulę:
A wstań jak wielkie posągi bezwstydne,
Naga – w styksowym wykąpana mule,

Would crush the heart of every Pole for shame.
I will not stand there before the spirit of Greece –
No, I would die first rather than go there in chains.

[14]
At Thermopylae – what would I say
If the knights rose before me on their grave,
And, showing me their bloodied chests,
Asked me plainly: "Were there many of you?
Forget the distance of long centuries between us."
If they asked me this – what would I say?

[15]
At Thermopylae a body lies
Without red cloak or golden sash.
It is the naked corpse of Leonidas:
A beautiful soul dwells in marble form.
For a long time the people mourned his sacrifice,
The scented flame and broken goblet.

[16]
O Poland! So long as your angelic soul
Is cased within a jovial skull,
So long will the executioner chop at your body,
Nor will your vengeful sword cause terror,
So long will you have a hyena prowling over you
And a grave to seize you – open-eyed!

[17]
Cast off the last shred of those hideous rags,
That burning shirt of Deianira:
And rise, unashamed, like great statues,
Naked – washed in the mire of the Styx,

Nowa – nagością żelazną bezczelna –
Niezawstydzona niczym – nieśmiertelna!

[18]
Niech ku pòłnocy z ciechej się mogiły
Podniesie naród i ludy przelęknie,
A tak hartowany, że w gromach nie pęknie,
Ale z piorunów ma ręce i wieniec,
Gardzący śmiercią wzrok – życia rumieniec.

[19]
Polsko! Lecz ciebie błyskotkami łudzą;
Pawiem narodów byłaś i papugą,
A teraz jesteś służebnicą cudzą.
Choć wiem, że słowa te nie zadrżą długo
W sercu – gdzie nie trwa myśl nawet godziny,
Mówię – bom smutny – i sam pełen winy.

[20]
Przeklnij – lecz ciebie przepędzi ma dusza
Jak eumenida – przez wężowe ròzgi,
Boś ty jedyny syn Prometeusza:
Sęp ci wyjada nie serce – lecz mòzgi.
Choć muzę moją w twojej krwi zaszargam,
Sięgnę do wnętrza twych trzew – i zatargam.

[21]
Szczeknij z boleści i przeklnij syna,
Lecz wiedz – że ręka przekleństw wyciągnięta
Nade mną –zwinie się w lęk jak gadzina
I z ramion ci się odkruszy zeschnięta,
I w proch ją czarne szatany rozchwycą;
Bo nie masz władzy przeklnąć – niewolnico!

New – insolent in iron nakedness –
Not shamed by anything – immortal!

[18]
Let the northern nation rise from its silent grave
And frighten other people at the sight,
Of such a huge statue – made from a single stone!
And so forged that it will never shatter in thunder,
But its hands and crown will be of lightning,
And a gaze scornful of death – its blush of life.

[19]
O Poland, you are still fooled by trinkets;
You have been the peacock and parrot of nations,
And now you are a foreign servant.
Although I know these words won't resonate long
In your heart – where thought does not stay for even an hour.
I say this because I am sad – and I myself am full of guilt.

[20]
Curse me – for my soul, like the Eumenides,
Runs you through a snaky gauntlet,
For you are Prometheus' only son:
The vulture doesn't eat your heart; it eats your brains.
Although I stain my muse with your blood,
I'll reach to your guts – and pull with all my might.

[21]
Put a curse on your son and howl in pain,
But be aware – the cursing hand
You stretch over me – will coil like a serpent
And snap off, withered, from your shoulder,
And then black devils will snatch it up from the dust;
For you have no power to curse – you slave!

[22]
Nie, nie, dopóki będziesz ręką drżącą
Zakrywać piersi puste, owdowiałe,
To ja nie klęknę, nawet przed klęczącą
Bo jam mam inną, smutną matkę – chwałę,
Co mi ociera łzy płynące rzadko,
A i tę trzecią mam . . . co mi jest matką . . .

[23]
O najbiedniejsza! Tobie z pòl myceńskich
Chciałbym już posłać prochòw moich urnę . . .
Wrzuć w proch ten – dwoje obrączek małżeńskich,
Zaklnij Dyjannę i duchy pochmurne,
Aby ci widziec mnie raz pozwoliły
W promieniach . . . jam ci był drogi i miły.

[24]
Teraz nie jestem niczym – a te mary,
Co okrażyły mnie . . . wzywają daléj
I pokazują girlandy i gwary
Anieslkich duchòw . . . Pójdę . . . krew mnie pali;
Już osadzony, śpiewam jak łabędzie,
Lecz gdy cię dojdzie pieśń, co z tobą będzie!

[25]
Tyś uśmiechała się – to było wczora,
Kiedyś mię smutnym w dzień znalazła inny
Zapłakanego – nad śmiercią Hektora.
Nie był to głupi płacz – ani dziecinny,
Głupsze sa teraz łzy . . . co lecą skorsze,
Gdy wspomnę los moj – ach! łzy stokroć gorsze.

[26]
Żurawie, co tam nad Koryntu gòrą

[22]
No, until with trembling hand
You cover your bare, widow's breast
I will not bend, even before a kneeling woman,
For I have another, sorrowful mother – glory –
Who dries the tears that seldom flow,
And there is a third one too whom I call mother . . .

[23]
O, my poorest mother! I would like to send you
An urn with my ashes from the fields of Mycenae . . .
Throw two wedding rings into these ashes,
Beseech Diana and her gloomy spirits
To allow you to see me one more time
In the moonbeams . . . for I was cherished by you.

[24]
Now I am nothing – but these ghosts
That surround me . . . swirl about
And point to the garlands and speak the cant
Of angelic spirits . . . I will go . . . my blood is burning;
Already judged, I sing like a swan,
But when my song arrives, what will happen to you!

[25]
You laughed – it seems like yesterday –
When you found me sad one time
And weeping over Hector's death.
These were not foolish tears, nor childish ones.
My tears are more foolish now . . . and flow more often,
When I recall my fate – ah, my tears are a hundred times
more bitter.

[26]
O cranes, forming your ranks toward the north

Rozciągnęłyście łańcuch ku północy,
Weźcie na skrzydła moję pieśń ponurą.
Zanieście z sobą . . . może przyszłej nocy
Kraj przelatywać będzie ta pieśń głucha,
Jak dzwon żałosny brzmiąc w krainach ducha.

[27]
Żurawie! Wy, co w powietrze ròżane
Co rana długą wzlatujecie szarfą,
Wyście mi były niegdyś ukochane,
Wyście jesienną moją były harfą!
Wy – i szumiące sosny nad grobami,
Gdzież się ja dzisiaj zobaczyłem z wami?

[28]
A jednak . . . jam to przeczuł w życia wiosnę,
Że będę kiedyś nieszczęsny i błędny . . .
Że może z serca niedoli urosnę
I będę z duchòw miał wieniec podrzędny,
I z dzika kiedyś pożegnam tęsknotą
Wasz łańcuch – zorzą pochłonięty złotą.

[29]
Dziś ta godzina przyszła . . . bądźcie zdrowe!
Tam Archipelag mnie woła błękitny,
Tam Korynt trzyma koronową głowę,
A za Lepantem Parnas starożytny . . .
O muzo moja! Jakże ty pozdrawiasz
Gòrę, gdzie siedział Apollo i Jowisz?

[30]
O romantyczna muzo, na kolana!
Bo ja ukłony mam tu dla tej góry
Od lipy wonnej klasycznego Jana

Above the mountain of Corinth,
Bear on your wings my gloomy song,
Carry it with you . . . maybe some night in the future
This hollow song will fly over my land
Like a bell lamenting in the world of the spirit.

[27]
O cranes! You, who in the rose-colored sky
Will rise in the morning like a trailing scarf,
You were once beloved of me,
You were my autumn harp!
You – and the pine trees rustling above the graves,
Where can I see you today?

[28]
And yet . . . I sensed even in the spring of life
That I would be unhappy one day and guilty . . .
That perhaps misfortune would grow from my heart
And I would not have the first crown among spirits,
And that one day, wild with sorrow,
I would leave you – engulfed in golden dawn.

[29]
Today your hour has come . . . be well!
There the gleaming archipelago calls me,
There Corinth keeps its crowned head,
And beyond the Lepanto ancient Parnassus rises . . .
O my muse! How should you greet
The mountain where Apollo and Zeus have sat?

[30]
O Romantic muse, on your knees!
For I will bow to this mountain
From the fragrant linden tree of classical Jan,

I od śpiewaka dzieci i tonsury,
I od śpiewaka Potockich ogrojca,
I cichy . . . łzawy pokłon mego ojca.

[31]
Ja wiem, że teraz on jest przy mnie duchem,
Ale mu twarda śmierć zamknęła wargi;
Oto mi nawet szczeleści nad uchem
Figowe drzewo . . . jakby – szmerem skargi . . .
Słyszę . . . głos mi już ojca niepamiętny,
Lecz jego musi to być głos – bom smętny.

[32]
Więc smutnym głosem i niedomòwionym
Pozwala czasem śmierć mòwić po śmierci.
Goro, co błyskasz księżycem czerwonym
Jak wulkan krwawy . . . O, pęknij na ćwierci . . .
Boś ty wyśmiana wròblòw świergotaniem
Albo za wczesnym rannych kuròw pianiem.

*   *   *   *   *   *   *   *   *   *   *   *   *   *   *

"Zachód Słońca nad Salaminą"

[20]
Biorę na świadki te strofy ostatnie,
Czy w nich poezji jest choć za trzy grosze.
Nie bòj sie, niech je twa krytyka płatnie –
Od nieprzyjaciòł moich więcej znoszę –
Te strofy sa złe, powiedz to otwarcie;
Pisałem, jakbym nigdy nie był w Sparcie;

From the fragrant linden tree of classical Jan,
And give a bow from the singer of the Potockis' garden
And I will send a quiet, tearful bow . . . from my father.

[31]
I know that now he is here with me in spirit,
Although harsh death has closed his eyes;
And the rustling of this fig tree
In my ear is like – the whisper of lips . . .
I hear . . . although I can no longer recall my father's
voice
This must be his voice – for it is sorrowful.

[32]
For sometimes death calls us even after death
In a sad and not quite audible voice.
O mountain, shining in the light of the red moon
Like a bloody volcano . . . o, break into bits . . .
For you are mocked by the sparrows' chirping
And the early morning crowing of the cock.

* * * * * * * * * * * * * * *

"Sunset over Salamis"

[20]
I call as my witnesses those last lines,
If they contain even a pennyworth of poetry
Don't be afraid, let your criticism pay the price –
I can take more from my enemies–
These lines are bad, so tell me so up front;
I wrote as if I'd never been in Sparta;

[21]
Te strofy są złe – no, więc na to zgoda;
Niepoetyczne... zgadzam sie i na to...
Chodźże tu do mnie... patrz... błękitna woda
Igra pod moją kaiką skrzydlata,
Łòdka przez falę rozbudzane pędzi
Jak najkształtniejszy z Olipmu łabędzi.

[22]
Przez nachylone żagle księżyc blady
Pokazuje mi majtki zadumane;
Stoją dawni rycerze Hellady,
O maszt oparci... złotem haftowane
Pancerze mają i białe kapoty...
Księżyc jest na nich błękitny i złoty.

[23]
Oni umieją zostać nieruchomi
Jako posągi, patrząc w niebo czyste,
Eol sam wichry szalone poskromi
I z żaglòw – muszle porobi srebrzyste,
W których się oni... na pòł skryci – mieszczą
Jak duchy – myślą wywołane wieszczą.

[24]
I cicho, i wraz... o godzino święta!
Łódka się w morskie rzuciła głębiny
I z jękiem nagle stanęła wzdrygnięta...
To była pierwsza fala Salaminy:
Spotkać pierwszego Polaka przybiegła
I wstrzęsła mnie tak... i jękła, i legła.

[25]
A za nią inne fale z wielkim gwarem

[21]
These lines are bad – here, I'll even grant it;
Unpoetic . . . I grant this too . . .
Come here to me . . . look . . . the shining water
Sports beneath my winged boat.
The boat breaks from the awakened wave
Like the most beautiful swan on Olympus.

[22]
The pale moon in the full sails
Shows me sailors lost in thought;
They stand like ancient knights of Hellas,
They lean on the mast . . . they have
Gilded spears and white cloaks . . .
The moon shines bright and gold upon them.

[23]
They know how to stay motionless
Like statues, looking at the clear sky;
Aeolus himself tames the furious winds,
And from their sails forms silvery shells,
In which they dwell, half-hidden,
Like spirits – freed by the thought of a bard.

[24]
It was quiet, and then suddenly – O blessed hour!
The boat pitched forward in the sea's depths
And with a groan suddenly shook . . .
This was the first wave of Salamis:
It ran up to meet its first Pole
And shook me hard . . . and groaned, and lay still.

[25]
And after it other waves ran up from the bank,

Od brzegu biegły, szerzące wzdychania.
Jutrzenka żywym spłonęła pożarem.
Słońce . . . już było bliskie swego wstania;
Myslałem, że w tym wiekopomnym kraju
Stanie w piorunach – jak Bòg na Synaju.

With a great roar, spreading with a sigh.
Dawn burst out with a vivid flame.
The sun shone . . . already bright from its ascent;
I thought that in this eternal land
It would rise in thunder – like God on Sinai.

Introduction

If Romantic poetry in Poland, taking root
in the rich soil of Slavic mythology and the traditions
of the North, were to embellish national literature
with as yet unknown splendor, to make it original and
accessible to simple people, why shouldn't we
extend its crown over another land and link
paganism with the Christian spirit of centuries . . .
Slavic Antiquity, the mythology of the North
and the spirit of the Middle Ages ought to be
the sources of Romantic poetry in Poland.

Maurycy Mochnacki, "On the Spirit and Sources of Poetry"
(Warsaw, 1825)[1]

The importance of Juliusz Słowacki (1809–1849) as Poland's
second greatest Romantic poet after Adam Mickiewicz (1798–
1856) is a well-established fact. Yet, in the English-speaking
world, Słowacki receives little more than honorable mention

1   Quoted from Alina Kowalczykowa, ed., *Idee programowe romantyków
     polskich*. Antologia [Programmatic Ideas of Polish Romantics. An
     Anthology], Biblioteka Narodowa (Wrocław: Zakład Narodowy im.
     Ossolińskich, 2000), pp. 96–97. All translations, unless otherwise noted,
     are our own.

even among students of Slavic literature.[2] Our intention is not to provide an overview of Słowacki's oeuvre, which can be gathered from any textbook on the history of Polish literature,[3] but to focus on Słowacki's use of Antiquity in his most famous lyric, *Agamemnon's Tomb* (1839). Our choice of this poem is dictated not just by its importance to Polish literature, but by its treatment of central themes in European Romanticism. Since Antiquity is an essential part of the fabric of Romantic poetry, *Agamemnon's Tomb* fits in our opinion best into the larger framework of European Romanticism out of all of Polish Romanticism. It is grounded in the ancient and therefore universal language of the epoch probably more than any other European Romantic poem. "If I am a poet, the air of Greece has made me one," Lord Byron once remarked. What is true of Byron is equally true of Słowacki and his literary output, where antique themes and elements flow like a torrent through virtually all his works.

For many, if not most, British and German poets (Schiller, Hölderlin, Byron, Shelley, Keats) Antiquity was a means of either discrediting the Christian world-view or introducing an aesthetic correction to it. For Słowacki, on the other hand, Antiquity was a yard-stick of measuring historical achievement and failure. What makes *Agamemnon's Tomb* unique, even when compared to the British or German Romantic

2 For example, in the extremely useful anthology edited by Michael Ferber, *European Romantic Poetry* (New York, Pearson Longman, 2005), the only Polish poet is Adam Mickiewicz. This anthology is the only one of its kind in English and is of incalculable value, but the absence of Słowacki is symptomatic. One should also mention here a recently published biography of Adam Mickiewicz by Roman Koropeckyj, *Adam Mickiewicz. The Life of a Romantic* (Ithaca & London: Cornell University Press, 2008).

3 See, for example, Czesław Miłosz, *The History of Polish Literature* (Berkeley: University of California Press, 1983).

literatures saturated with ancient themes,[4] is that it harnesses Antiquity as an interpretative mirror for Słowacki's understanding of the history of Poland and assessing the Polish national character. "What is the poem about?" asks one of Słowacki's scholars. "Agamemnon's tomb? Not at all. The Masterly picture of 'the underground dome – built on the blood of the cruel Atreides' and the feeling of concentration, which the dome entices in him – is a small and silent prelude to the tempest of emotions which follows it . . . [when the poet presents] himself to his nation as its bard, summoning it to a new path."[5]

Leaving aside the obvious problem of properly rendering poetry in another language, the historical entanglement of Polish Romanticism explains why there is hardly any familiarity with Polish Romanticism outside of Poland.[6] However, what is true of most poems of Polish Romanticism does not have to be the case with *Agamemnon's Tomb*. Słowacki's ingenuity in this poem lies in his weaving the parochialism of national history into the tapestry of the universal language of Greek Antiquity. For this very reason Słowacki is closer to being understood by non-Polish audiences than his great contemporary Adam Mickiewicz.

In assessing the role of Greece's influence on Słowacki, a distinguished Polish classicist and a passionate connoisseur of

4   The scholarly literature on the influence of classics on Romantic literature in particular is immense and easily available. One should consult, however, two well known accounts: Gilbert Highet, *The Classical Tradition. Greek and Roman Influences on Western Literature* (New York/Oxford: A Galaxy Book, 1957) and Douglas Bush, *Mythology and the Romantic Tradition in English Poetry* (Cambridge: Harvard University Press, 1937).

5   Józef Tretiak, *Juliusz Słowacki*, 2 vols. (Kraków: Akademia Umiejętności, 1904), vol. 1, pp. 108–109.

6   Even in France, a country traditionally culturally closer to Poland than any other, Słowacki's "Agamemnon's Tomb" was translated by Roger Legras only in 2001.

Słowacki's works, Tadeusz Sinko, states: "Influences of all romantic literatures which proclaimed a cult of Greece are fused in Słowacki's Hellenism. It is only against their background that his Hellenism ceases to be something extraordinary and becomes something necessary and essential to it."[7] Originally composed as the eighth canto in his verse travelogue *Voyage to the Holy Land*, the first 21 stanzas of the poem were published separately along with Słowacki's historical-mythic drama, *Lilla Weneda*, an account of the origins of the Polish state, based overtly on Greek tragedy.[8] *Voyage to the Holy Land* was never completed, and *Agamemnon's Tomb* was the only part of it publicly recited and published in Słowacki's lifetime. It stands independently as a statement about Poland and its relation to Greece, but it also needs to be read with *Lilla Weneda* because Słowacki placed them together.[9] Last, when read in the context that Słowacki first intended it – embedded

7   Tadeusz Sinko, *Hellenizm Juliusza Słowackiego* [Juliusz Słowacki's Hellenism] (Warsaw: Instytut Wydawniczy "Biblioteka Polska," 1925), p. 49.

8   Short fragments of the play were translated by Michael Mikoś in his anthology of Słowacki's works: *Juliusz Słowacki, This Fateful Power. Sesquicentennial Anthology 1809–1849* (Lublin: Norbertinum, 1999), pp. 112–121.

9   In the Preface to *Balladina*, Słowacki writes: "For how often it was that I would gaze at the ruins of the old castle that stood on a hill overlooking my hometown [Krzemieniec], and dream that one day I would populate the ring of shattered walls with specters, spirits and knights; that I would rebuild the broken chambers and would illuminate them with the fire of lightning-filled evenings, and would command the ceilings to repeat the ancient Sophoclean *alas*" (trans. by Bill Johnston, in *Poland's Angry Romantic* [Cambridge Scholars Publishing: Cambridge, 2009], p. 32; *Dzieła*, vol. II, p. 332). ("Alas" is a references to Sophocles' *Electra*, where the heroine Electra in her conversation with her brother Orestes, who has not yet revealed his identity, repeats "alas" five times: ll. 1115, 1179, 1184, 1210, 1246.). What sounds at first like a young boy's dream later becomes real: Słowacki turned his poetic gift into a tool of national transformation by resuscitating Greek tragedy in *Lilla Weneda* and

in a travelogue in verse full of sparkling commentary and allusions, in the tradition established by Chateaubriand, Lamartine and Byron – we may speculate on the poet's train of thought as he developed his reflections on Greek Antiquity and contemporary Poland. The two texts are in fact significantly different, as the published poem ends after stanza 21, the climax of the poet's castigation of Poland. The last eleven stanzas that were found in the manuscript provide a very different tone and moral to the ending of the poem. This commentary is the first work on *Agamemnon's Tomb* that is concerned with the whole poem, not merely individual stanzas. Finally, we are not only providing a commentary on the whole poem, but are reading it against the background of contemporary context and ancient sources.[10]

Agamemnon's Tomb. In commenting on the relationship between *Agamemnon's Tomb*, *Lilla Weneda* and *Balladina*, Maria Kalinowska rightly notes that Słowacki "in a sense repeats the Greek miracle of the birth of tragedy [. . .] throwing a bridge between archaic Greece and the most ancient Poland. This is a repetition of what had happened at the very source of Greek tragedy [. . .] In such paradoxically created images of South and North can one notice an echo of Romantic arguments over the Polish national character and over Poland's belonging to two opposite camps; we also hear echoes of disputes over the ancient origins of Polish history." ("Słowackiego Greckie Sny o Polsce" [Słowacki's Greek Dreams about Poland], in Juliusz Słowacki – Poeta Europejski [Juliusz Słowacki – A European Poet], ed. by Maria Cieśla-Korytowska, Włodzimierz Szturc, Agnieszka Ziołowicz [Kraków: Universitas, 2000], pp. 24, 20).

10   This work owes more than we can express in footnotes to the labor of Tadeusz Sinko (1877–1966). Sinko was a Polish classicist who, in addition to his scholarly output on Antiquity, which comprises about 800 books, articles, and editions of ancient writers, made it his "hobby" to trace the influences of Antiquity in Polish literature. The fruit of his incredibly detailed labor was a number of books without which the present commentary would be impossible. The ones that we benefited from the most are: *Hellenizm Juliusza Słowackiego* [Juliusz Słowacki's Hellenism] (1925), *Antyk w "Król-Duch"* [Antiquity in "Krol-Duch"]

(1910), *Hellada i Roma w Polsce* [Hellas and Roma in Poland] (1933), *Od Olimpu do Olimpji* [From Olympus to Olympia] (1928), *Echa klasyczne w literaturze polskiej* [Classical Echos in Polish Literature] (1923), *Mickiewicz i antyk* [Mickiewicz and Antiquity] (1957), *Antyk Wyspiańskiego* [Wyspiański's Antiquity] (1922), *Rapsody Historyczne St. Wyspianskiego* [St. Wyspiański's Historical Rhapsodies] (1924). Curiously enough, Sinko never provided a sustained reading of *Agamemnon's Tomb* against the references that he found in ancient texts. Maria Kalinowska, "Parallels Between Greece and Poland in Juliusza Slowacki's Oeuvre, pp. 207–221, in: A Handbook to Classical Reception in Eastern and Central Europe. Edited by Zara Martirosova Torlone, Dana LaCourse Munteanu and Dorota Dutsch. Oxford, Willey Blackwell, 2017. Also worthy of mention are the heavy-weight "French/German" style work of scholarship on Słowacki's Antiquity by Wanda Amarantidou, *Juliusz Słowacki i Grecja Nowożytna* [Juliusz Słowacki and Modern Greece] (Łódź: Wydawnictwo Uniwersytetu Łódzkiego, 2006).

The history of classical education and classical background of the Polish Romantics is discussed by Leon T. Błaszczyk, "The Mickiewicz Generation and the Classical Heritage: A Contribution to the Study of Polish Neo-Humanism," in Victor Terras, ed., *American Contributions to the Eighth International Congress of Slavists. Zagreb and Ljubljana, September 3–9, 1978*. Vol. 2. Literature (Columbus, OH: Slavica, 1978), and T. Sinko in *Hellada i Roma w Polsce*, pp. 6–23.

Historical Background

An overview of the historical context of Polish Romanticism is indispensable for following the argument of *Agamemnon's Tomb*.

In 1795 Poland disappeared from the map of Europe; it was gone for a hundred and twenty-three years until, in 1918, it regained its independence. In 1795 its territories were divided among three neighboring powers: Russia, Prussia and Austria. The partitions occurred in three successive acts: August 5, 1772; January 23, 1793; and October 24, 1795. The developments that led to this unprecedented act of erasing a country from the political map of Europe were twofold: the growing power of Poland's neighbors on the one hand and the increasing internal weakness of the Polish state on the other.

The catastrophe of 1795 was "prophesied" by a Polish king himself, Jan III Sobieski – the victorious hero who stopped the Turkish invasion of Europe in 1683. In his speech to the Polish Senate in March 1688, Sobieski said:

> Future generations will wonder in astonishment that after such resounding victories, such international triumph and glory, we now face, alas, eternal shame and irreversible

loss, for we now find ourselves without resources, help-less, and seemingly incapable of government.[1]

Sobieski is referring to the (in)famous *liberum veto* ("I freely say No") in Polish law; according to the Polish constitution, every parliamentary decision required absolute unanimity; one contrary vote meant that the decision did not have sufficient support. *Liberum veto* was an extreme extension of the principle of consensus, whose origin can be traced to a legal act of 1505, *Nihil novi*,[2] which was designed to limit royal power. *Nihil novi* is short for *Nihil novi nisi commune consensus* ("Nothing new without the consensus of all").[3] This act is considered to be the beginning of Poland's status as a so-called "Nobles' Democracy." The nobility had an extraordinary amount of power, including their unique right to elect the king, a right that is often referred to as the Golden Liberty.

1   Quoted in Adam Zamoyski. *The Polish Way. A Thousand-Year History of the Poles and Their Culture* (New York: Franklin Watts, 1988), p. 206.

2   Andrzej Walicki notes that the principle of *unanimitas*, which goes back to the English jury system or cardinals' conclave, can be interpreted either as the physical or moral subjugation of an individual to the community, or an expression of individualism, as was the case of Poland. See Walicki, *The Slavophile Controversy. History of a Conservative Utopia in Nineteenth-Century Russian Thought* (Notre Dame: University of Notre Dame Press, 1989), pp. 262–263.

3   The text reads: "Since general laws and public acts apply not to a single person but to the whole nation, therefore at this general diet in Radom, together with all prelates, councils and land deputies of our kingdom, we have considered rightful and just, as well as decided, that from now on nothing new may be decided by us and our successors, without a common consensus of senators and land deputies, that would be detrimental or burdensome to the Commonwealth (Rzeczpospolita/Res publica) or harmful or injurious to anyone, or that would alter the general law and public freedom."

Although the Constitution was of course not intentionally designed to sabotage the political process – and in fact it worked well for 147 years, until the first veto was used – in theory it made it possible for a single nobleman to veto a treaty, an agreement, taxation, or a reform proposal. *Liberum veto* was used for the first time in 1652, again in 1669, and next in 1679. The *liberum veto* could and in fact did become a practical weapon for foreign powers to intervene in Poland's internal affairs. In one case when the veto was going to be abolished in 1667, Brandenburg and Sweden even agreed to go to war "in defense of Polish freedoms."

By the late 18th century the political disease was too advanced to reform the country. As Adam Zamoyski writes: "The spectacle of a society galloping towards its own destruction is incomprehensible and irritating to the modern mind conditioned by the orthodoxies of nationalism and progress. The very existence of the *liberum veto*, that most powerful symbol of the [Polish-Lithuanian] Commonwealth's political decay, leads many to conclude that the Poles had parted with their senses."[4] A group of reformers tried to reverse the decay by designing a new Constitution, announced on May 3, 1791. The Constitution introduced political equality between the nobility and townspeople and made provisions for protecting the peasantry. Most importantly, the Constitution abolished *liberum veto*. Its adoption provoked the hostility of Catherine the Great, who allied herself with the so-called Targowica Confederation composed of Polish Magnates, who, seeing in it a limitation of their privileges, opposed the reforms. The Targowica came to be known as a symbol of national treason.

The swan song of dying Poland was the Kościuszko

---

4   A. Zamoyski, *The Polish Way*, p. 207. See also Józef Andrzej Gierowski, "The International Position of Poland in the Seventeenth and Eighteenth Centuries," in J. K. Fedorowicz, ed. and trans., *A Republic of Nobles. Studies in Polish History to 1864* (Cambridge: Cambridge University Press, 1981), pp. 218–238.

Insurrection of 1794. On March 24, 1794, General Tadeusz Kościuszko, a hero of the American War of Independence, swore an oath on the Market Square in Kraków, in which he promised to recover the Commonwealth's borders, sovereignty and freedom. The Polish army was defeated on October 10 at Maciejowice the same year. On October 24, 1795, the last partition took place and Poland ceased to exist as a political entity, and regained its independence only after one hundred twenty three years. The Napoleonic wars awakened hopes among Poles. Many of those who were scattered all over Europe joined the French Emperor, hoping that his victory over the occupying powers would allow them to regain their country's independence. In 1807 Napoleon created the Duchy of Warsaw from the territories ceded from Prussia by the treaty of Tilsit. However, after Napoleon's defeat, Prussia and Russia divided the Duchy at the Congress of Vienna, and created the semi-independent Congress Kingdom, which was much smaller than the Duchy. Again, the Congress Kingdom was short-lived. It ceased to exist in 1831 after the failure of the Polish November Uprising against Russia, which was Poland's last realistic hope to regain independence. The Uprising made Russia seek the most extreme measures, sending 80,000 Poles, including many aristocrats, to Siberia.[5]

5   "In Lithuania and Ukraine the punitive measures were on an industrial scale. General Muravyov, nicknamed 'Hangman Muravyov' by the Russians (not the Poles), rampaged the countryside stringing people up and burning whole villages on the mere whiff of a suspicion of sympathy for the Polish cause. In Podolia, 5,000 families of minor szlachta [nobility] were dispossessed of everything, degraded to peasant status and transported to Siberia; the families of szlachta from Lithuania and Volhynia were conveyed to Siberia in the same fashion. The accent was on humiliating the proud, degrading the noble, removing the vertebrae. Prince Roman Sanguszko, who was of Rurik's blood and might have qualified for some respect in Russia, was sentenced to hard labor for life in Siberia and made to walk there chained to a gang of convicts" (A. Zamoyski, *The Polish Way*, p. 275).

Four years later, visiting Warsaw, Tsar Nicholas reminded the Poles:

> You have, gentlemen, a choice between two eventualities: to persist in your illusion concerning an independent Poland, or to live quietly as loyal subjects under my rule. If you persist in your dreams of a separate nation, of an independent Poland, and of all chimeras of this kind, you will only draw great hardships upon yourselves. I have ordered a citadel to be constructed here, and I declare that on the slightest demonstration I will destroy the city – and it certainly will not be I who will restore it . . .[6]

These were the political conditions for the emergence of Polish Romanticism. Literature became a means of protecting national identity and writers were not mere versifiers but national bards. Their message was never solely poetic but also social and political. And of all poems created in Europe during the Romantic period, Słowacki's *Agamemnon's Tomb* is one of the best examples of a poem where poetry, historical themes, and the moral evaluation of a national character are fused into one.

6   Quoted in W. Lednicki, "Mickiewicz at the College de France, 1840–1940," *Slavonic Year-Book. American Series*, Vol. 1 (1941), p. 151.

Part 1.
Poetic Background of Słowacki's Agamemnon's Tomb.

The structure of Słowacki's *Agamemnon's Tomb* is reminiscent of Dante's *Divine Comedy* which he very likely took as his model.[1] It is part of a larger poem, *Voyage to the Holy Land*, where the poet recounts his journey to Egypt, Greece, and Turkey. Słowacki is also drawing upon a tradition of British and French Romanticism, following poetically in the footsteps of Byron, Lamartine, and Chateaubriand. However, what for Lamartine was an exercise in the geography of landscape, with no interest in Greek architecture; what for Chateaubriand was a series of reflections on the collapse of ancient civilizations; and what for Byron was a call for the Greeks to regain their ancient heritage against the Muslim Turks, for Słowacki was an attempt to read the history or fate of his country against the

---

1   For structural similarities and Dante's influence on Słowacki's poems (on "Piast Dantyszek" in particular), see Juljusz Kleiner, *Juljusz Słowacki. Dzieje Twòrczosci* [*Juliusz Słowacki. A History of His Poetry*], 2 vols. (Lwów-Warszawa-Kraków: Wydawnictwo Zakładu Narodowego im. Ossolińskich, 1924), vol. 2, p. 153ff.

history of ancient Greece. But there is more to Słowacki's *Agamemnon's Tomb* than a reflection on Poland's past. While Chateaubriand dismissed the idea that the modern Greeks shared anything with their ancient predecessors, Słowacki, like Byron, believed in the possibility of resurrecting the ancient Greek spirit and harnessing it in the service of Messianism, a doctrine equating the fate of a nation with Christian ideas of the sacrifice and salvation of Christ. *Agamemnon's Tomb*, plus several other Cantos from his *Voyage to the Holy Land* and a few other related poems written around the same period, constitute fairly coherent material for Słowacki's Messianic vision of Poland. Unlike Mickiewicz, who put forth his Messianism in his *Books of the Polish Pilgrims*, Słowacki never devoted a single work to expound his Messianic ideas.[2] His thoughts on the subject are scattered throughout his writings, but they are numerous enough to realize how strong his messianic streak was. However, what sets his Messianism apart from that of his fellow countryman is that Słowacki's Messianism is entirely permeated by Greek thought.

Approached from this angle, *Agamemnon's Tomb*, despite its overtly Greek character, inscribes itself within a Christian religious framework. There is no Messiah in the poem, but there is Prometheus; there is no sin or corruption, but there is

2   Mickiewicz's Messianism and its influence on others is very well discussed by Lednicki, "Mickiewicz at the College de France," p. 151. See also Andrzej Walicki, *Philosophy and Romantic Nationalism. The Case of Poland* (Notre Dame: The University of Notre Dame Press,1994). When discussing Messianism in his massive study, *Political Messianism. The Romantic Phase* (New York: Frederick A. Praeger, 1960), Jacob Talmon (who knew Polish) devoted an entire chapter to Mickiewicz without mentioning, for example, Słowacki. See also Talmon's discussion of Messianism in *Romanticism and Revolt. Europe 1815–1848* (New York: Norton & Company, 1967). Many scholars address Mickiewicz's Messianism but treat Słowacki's only slightly at best.

the crime of patricide that is exposed and needs to be atoned for; there is no salvation, but there is hope of the awakening of the sleeping Greek warriors in Słowacki's *Sunrise over Salamis*, which could very well be the intended ending to *Agamemnon's Tomb*. Again, there is no death and resurrection of the Messiah, but there are indications that Poland, "crucified" in the act of partition by Prussia, Russia and Austria, can appropriate the Greek Spirit, making itself a savior of nations.

Part 2.

"Sing, O Muse": In the footsteps of Aeneas and Electra

[1]
Let my magically strung lute
Resound more gloomily and more darkly,
For I have entered Agamemnon's tomb,
And I sit quietly in the underground dome
Caked in the blood of the cruel Atreides.
My heart is asleep, but still it dreams. How sad I am!

[2]
O! How far off sounds that golden harp,
Whose eternal echo is all that I hear!
This is a druidic grotto of great stones,
Where the wind comes in to sigh in the cracks
And brings me Electra's voice: she whitens the wash
And calls me from the laurel trees: "How sad I am!"

    The poet begins by invoking a particular kind of darkness,
one "built on blood," sounding the theme of cruelty and crime.
At first, the silence and sleep appear to be attributes of the poet,

not the place. There is a striking paradox: his heart, the realm of emotions, is asleep (suggesting that his emotional life is not functioning), yet at the same time he is experiencing an emotion that is the function of the heart: he is "sad." This discrepancy suggests that sorrow is a state obtained when the heart is not working. Perhaps sleep releases the heart's emotions and allows for poetic creativity. As in his invocation to the "Romantic Muse" at the beginning of the *Voyage*, where he follows established tropes of the romantic travelogue only to dismiss them, the poet here is trying to find the true conditions for romantic inspiration.

The idea of a voice originating in the leaves of the laurel tree conjures up three major associations. The first is Virgil's *Aeneid* (Bk. III: ll. 30–73), where Polydorus, Priam's son, who was betrayed and killed by a traitor ally of Troy who joined Agamemnon, speaks to Aeneas from the trees. Aeneas releases Polydorus' voice by picking branches for a sacrifice: "I tried to tear some green shoots from the brush . . . when a dreadful, ghastly sight, too strange for words, strikes my eyes" (ll. 30–33).[1] Aeneas' pulling at the tree roots causes Polydorus' blood to flow. The inadvertent and unintended act of violence Aeneas commits anticipates other references to tearing and shaking of trees. In Dante's *Inferno* (canto XIII), the bleeding tree symbolizes the sin of suicide. Last, in Ovid, numerous metamorphoses take the form of trees: in the case of Daphne (Bk. I, ll. 335–366) the transformation saves her from the unwanted love of Apollo: she becomes the laurel tree, an image which features prominently in Słowacki's poem. In another of the "metamorphoses," the story of Myrrha, the woman is turned into a myrrh tree for the crime of incest (Bk. X, 312 ff.; 489 ff).

The only person who answers Słowacki's call in the empty tomb in stanza 2 is Electra, who echoes his phrase, "I am sad."

---

1   Virgil, The *Aeneid*, trans. Robert Fagels (New York: Viking, 2006).

Her repetition of his thoughts establishes a kinship between them, a motif that will recur later. In Sophocles' play *Electra*, the mournful heroine meets her brother Orestes but does not know who he is: the young princess complains about the menial work her mother has forced her to do and Orestes tells her he shares in her mourning.[2] We have an array of associations here: Electra's complaints bring her brother Orestes on the scene to avenge their father's death. This throws us into the midst of the ancient tragedy of the house of Atreides. The crime of the Atreides family is complex and layered: Agamemnon is forced to sacrifice his daughter Iphigenia at Artemis' command for crossing her sanctuary in pursuit of a deer;[3] to avenge the death of their daughter, Clytemnestra murders him upon his return from Troy; their children, Electra and Orestes, are obliged in turn to murder Clytemnestra in revenge; Orestes is finally driven mad by the Eumenides (who are invoked by Słowacki later in the poem, in stanza 24), for having committed the crime of matricide.

The Polish phrase here "bieli płótno" can be rendered in several ways: "starches" or "whitens linen." On the surface the expression appears to be no more than an allusion to manual labor unbecoming for a princess. However, in his letter to the

2   Electra answers her brother's question, "Who is it that forces you to such subjection?" with: "She is called my mother – but like a mother in nothing." Orestes, disguised, exclaims "Poor girl! When I look at you, how I pity you." Electra responds: "Then you are the only one that ever pitied me"; Orestes: "Yes. I alone came here and felt your pain." Sophocles, *Electra*, ll. 1190 ff. (in Sophocles II, trans. David Grene, (Chicago: University of Chicago Press, 1969), p. 172).

3   Słowacki invokes Iphigenia in Canto IV ("Greece"), stanza 53: "A wielkie morze, lazurowe morze,/Któremu niegdyś poświęcono w Aulis/Córy królewskie . . ." ("And the great sea, the azure sea,/ to which at one time the king's daughters were sacrificed at Aulis").

poet Zygmunt Krasiński, Słowacki uses the same phrase but qualifies what kind of cloth the word "płótno" refers to: "You, spirits said, whom we saw in the dark tomb of Agamemnon; you who once rode along the banks of the laurel stream where the Princess Electra washed her mother's clothes."[4] (In none of the three ancient tragedians do we find a reference to Electra washing her mother's clothes.[5]) In the *Electra* of Słowacki's "beloved Euripides" we find a scene to which Słowacki may be alluding. The scene occurs after the killing of their mother by Orestes:

Electra:
I urged you on, I urged you on,
I touched the sword beside your hand.

Chorus:
Working a terrible pain and ruin.

Orestes:
Take it! shroud my mother's dead flesh in my cloak,
Clean and close the sucking wounds.
You carried your own death in your womb.

4   "Lecz ty, mówiły dalej mary, któregośmy widziały w ciemnym Agamemnona grobowcu; Ty jadący niegdyś brzegami laurowego potoku, gdzie Elektra kròlewan płótno bieliła matczyne." 2nd Letter to [Z. Krasiński] the author of Irydjon. Słowacki, *Dzieła* [Works], vol. VII, p. 287–288.

5   "Washing linen" may not necessarily be low work for a person of Electra's status: recall that in Homer's *Odyssey* Nausica, the daughter of King Alcinous, finds Odysseus when she goes to the shore to wash clothes: "Come, let's go wash theses clothes at the break of day." Book 6, ll. 34–35. *The Odyssey*, Translated by Robert Fagles, with Introduction and Notes by Bernard Knox *New York: Viking, 1996.*

Electra:
Behold! I wrap her close in the robe,
The one I loved and could not love. (ll. 1225–1231)[6]

Read with an eye to this passage, "bieli płótno *matczyne*" brings to mind – not surprisingly, given the context of Słowacki's reflection on Agamemnon's death – the murder of the mother whose shroud Electra washes in the neighboring river. Another interpretative possibility, which stresses the connection between Greek tragedies and Słowacki's own tragedy *Lilla Weneda*, is that the Electra of the Greek tragedians serves as an associative link to Słowacki's own heroine Lilla, who in Słowacki's play says:

Ja przyszłam twoje nogi rosić łzami,
Ja będę twoją sługą; będę
Płótno bielić, twoje krowy doić.

I came to wash your feet with my tears
I shall be your servant; I shall
Wash the linen; I shall milk your cows. (ll. 280–284)

However, because Lilla washes "feet with her tears" in addition to washing linen, the obvious reference in this passage is to a sinful woman from the New Testament – often associated with Mary Magdalene – who washes Christ's feet with her own tears (Luke 7: 36–50). This mixture of symbolism from Greek tragedies and the Christian New Testament can be explained by the context of Słowacki's play about the ancient origin of *Christian* Poland. Słowacki joined the pre-Christian and Christian symbolic systems by injecting Christian humility into Greek tragedy – and turning a defiant Greek matricide into a humble Christian Lilla.

6   *Electra*, translated by Emily Townsend Vermuele, in *Euripides V* (Chicago & London: The University of Chicago Press, 1968).

Słowacki's description of the family of Atreides as a "house of crime" indicates his approach to Poland and Polish history: Słowacki claimed he found Polish history insufficiently bloody.[7] Although it is not an historical novel but a tragedy à la grec, his creation of a Polish mythic past in *Lilla Weneda*, where an entire tribe is wiped out, can be seen as Słowacki's attempt to present Polish history in a tragic way. Besides, the link between *Agamemnon's Tomb* and *Lilla Weneda* (to which *Agamemnon's Tomb* was published as an epilogue) suggests that the poem is a recasting of Polish history in Greek dress.[8] One possible way of imposing a Greek reading of the initial scene is to say that when Electra responds to the poet's call she is calling upon Słowacki to avenge her father's death. This makes Słowacki an Orestes figure whose role is to become the avenger of their father. In a later stanza Słowacki will in fact assume the role of an avenger. In Polish there is only one name for fatherland and motherland: *ojczyzna* (fatherland), and the poem is in fact about the death of the *father*land and the distribution of guilt.

7   "La Pologne est jusqu'a present une mine vierge pour les ecrivains des romans historiques. – Son histoire presente peu de faits sanguinaires – c'est un champ ou l'ecrivain de romans recolte lorsque un poete tragique est obliger de glaner" (Until now Poland has been virgin soil for the writers of historial novels. Its history presents too few bloody events– this is a field where the novelist harvests while a tragic poet is obliged to glean.) *Le Roi de Ladawa. Roman Historique de la Derniere Revolution de Pologne.* Słowacki, *Dzieła* [Works] (Wrocław: Wydawnictwo Zakładu Narodowego im. Ossolińskich, 1952), vol. XI, p. 11. All references to Słowacki's works are to this edition.

8   As we pointed out earlier, the thematic connection between *Agamemnon's Tomb* and *Lilla Weneda* has been forcefully and convincingly argued for by Maria Kalinowska: "Słowackiego Greckie Sny o Polsce" ["Słowacki's Greek Dreams about Poland"] in: *Juliusz Słowacki –Poeta Europejski* [Juliusz Słowacki –A European Poet], ed. Maria Cieśla-Korytowska, Włodzimierz Szturc, and Agnieszka Ziołowicz (Kraków: Universitas, 2000), pp. 15–28.

The dark silence associated with Electra is the muffling of outside noises in the tomb. The joyful song suggested by the "golden harp" is very far away from the poet – although he can still hear it. The specificity of the location, the massive stones, the laurel trees, is disrupted by the non-Mediterranean epithet "druidic," a word that evokes northern (Celtic) pagan religion. Here we have the first hint that the southern (Greek) topography is linked to the northern topography that is later (stanzas 26 and 27) associated with ancient Poland. The northern motif helps account for the attachment of this poem to the mythological tragedy *Lilla Weneda*.[9]

The link between the play and the poem has been pointed out many times. But what exactly did Słowacki mean by including the two works in a single volume for publication? The idea of *Lilla Weneda* was to present dramatically an historical myth of the origins of Poland. In the Romantic period there was a trend to recreate the national past in order to define the specificity of the national culture; folklore and ancient national history was a common means of achieving this.[10] Słowacki knew of one of the newer histories of Poland firsthand. His Parisian neighbor, Frederyk Henryk Lewestam, had written

9   "Druidic" does not seem a particularly Polish word, as it denotes a specifically Celtic religion. However, it does suggest the oak tree (from the Greek *drusis*), and thus symbolizes the North. Moreover, in other works of Polish Romanticism, Celtic and Germanic are fused with "Slavic" in opposition to the southern races of Rome and Greece: for example, in *Iridion*, by Zygmunt Krasiński, the Scandinavian, Celtic and Germanic are blended into Slavic. The gladiator in Byron's *Childe Harold*, a Dacian or a Goth, is translated in Polish by Słowacki's contemporary and critic Bogdan Zaleski as "Slav" (słowianin).

10 So great was the need for a unique past and poetic tradition that several forgeries were famously created to fill the void: most famously the "Scottish" Ossian and two Czech epics were contemporary inventions; even the authenticity of the Russian *Tale of Igor's Campaign* is still disputed by scholars.

Pierwotne dzieje polski (*The Earliest History of Poland*) in 1839. The book was published later, but when Lewestam was writing it he spoke with Słowacki often. Thus Słowacki wrote *Lilla Weneda* and *Agamemnon's Tomb* with direct knowledge of Lewestam's theory of the Polish nation. Słowacki's familiarity with Lewestam and his work has been written about by Stanisław Turowski, whose findings are worth briefly presenting here.[11] According to Lewestam, the Polish nobility came from the Lechs (Lechici). The Slavs (Słowianie, written Sławianie by Lewestam) and the Celts lived together and mixed; hence the name Ligurowie: "lid gòr," i.e., people of the mountains. The Slavs were good-tempered, docile (łagodni) and good. They did not know class difference. They succumbed to the power of the Celtic conquerors. The thesis Lewestam makes, bolstered by many ingenious (but probably dubious) etymological links between the Celtic and Polish languages, is that Celts are forerunners of the Polish gentry, a rough ("rubaszny") conquering tribe. Some of his linguistic "evidence" for the link between Celtic and Polish were clearly exploited by Słowacki in his works: the word "pan" ("lord," contemporary "mister"), writes Lewestam, comes from the Celtic word "ban," which means powerful, highbrow (wzniosly). Celtic "Llach" means "bright/glittering"; "lleach," or "llech," means "free/separate." The word Polak (Polish man, Pole) means "po Lachu" (after Lach); "szlachcic/slachcic" (nobleman) comes from z-lach-cic (that is, born of Lach), because -cic is a patronymic ending. Lachowie or Llechowie are the people who are the beginning of Poland, and are the high nobility without belonging to any Slavonic branch. A Lach is flexible (swift), fiery, entrepreneurial, jovial, a true warrior's

---

11 See Stanisław Turowski, "Geneza narodu polskiego w 'Lilli Wenedzie'" ["Genesis of the Polish Nation in 'Lilla Weneda'"], in *Pamiętnik Literacki*, 1909, 170–188.

son, but also able to improve himself; a Slav is slow, just, mild as a child, attached to his customs, however, he is passive.

Lewestam's book fits an early 19th century historiographical pattern, according to which the conquering tribes are violent, brutal, rough and lack in "sophistication."[12] Yet the details in Lewestam's theory shed particular light on *Lilla Weneda* and *Agamemnon's Tomb*. For example, his mythic use of Celts to signify northern Europeans explains the attribute "druidic" in the opening stanzas of *Agamemnon's Tomb*: it returns the poet to the north, to the pre-historic Polish world of *Lilla Weneda*. In addition, Słowacki departs from contemporary historiography in the conclusion of his poem, where the noble and poetic Weneds (Venedi or Veneti, referred to by Tacitus, *Annalas*, Bk. XI, and other Roman authors, were people living along Vistula river in Poland) are completely annihilated as a race by the Lechs.[13]

Słowacki's juxtaposition of the two tribes seems to have an explanatory goal. The Lechs represent the vices characteristic of the later Polish nobility that led to Poland's destruction; the conquered Weneds represent the "angelic" soul of Poland: innocence and virtue. As one of the characters in the play, Ślaz, says, summarizing his own (national) character:

12   For that matter, French historiography posits a similar mixing of two races, one indigenous, peaceful, and cultured, and the other violent and brutal. Słowacki would have known from the histories of Julius Caesar and *Les Martyrs* by Chateaubriand that Celts were supposedly related to the Gauls (the French). See Turowski, *ibid.*, pp. 180 ff. For a contemporary, very discerning historical account of the early history of Poland, see Norman Davies, *God's Playground. A History of Poland*, vol. I (New York: Columbia University Press, 1982), chapter 2, pp. 23–60. For an account of French historians' attempts at that time to determine their own protohistory, see Highet, *The Classical Tradition*, pp. 477–478.

13   Turowski, ibid., p. 171. T. Sinko (*Hellenizm Juliusza Słowackiego*, p. 192) remarks that if Słowacki made any use of ancient tragedies in composing his play, the only one that could have inspired him was Euripides' *The Trojan Women*, where the whole nation is destroyed.

Am I a Lech; why? Boorishness, gluttony, drunkenness,
Seven deadly sins, proneness to yelling,
And even a fondness for pickled cucumbers, ancestors'
crests;
The habit to swear in verba magistri;
Shepherdess, do I have all this written on my forehead?

Ślaz's words are a summary of what Słowacki terms
"rubaszność" in *Agamemnon's Tomb*.[14] On the other hand, the
Lechs are "good at fighting and hunting but not at what is boring." (The latter being probably a reference to poetry and
thoughtful reflection.) The Weneds, on the other hand, are innocent, motivated by heart and harp; they represent a dreamy people
inspired by hope and poetry. However, national survival requires
a combination of sword, plough, harp and heart.[15] As Manfred
Kridl notes, the Weneds die at the end, and thus their "angelic
soul," a term that Słowacki uses in *Agamemnon's Tomb*, cannot
be a reference to anything living in Słowacki's contemporaries.[16]
The end of the Weneds is supposed to refer to the "historically"
failed attempt to meld contradictory elements "into one."
    Another element that connects the two works is the motif
of the harp, a vehicle for poetry and national memory. In stanza
1 in *Agamemnon's Tomb* we observe the transformation of a
Greek lyre or lute into a Celtic or northern harp that links the

14 This also corresponds to Zygmunt Krasiński's ideas about Poland, quoted below in this study.
15 See Janina Kamionkowa, "Romantyczne dzieje sterotypu Sarmaty" ["Romantic Vicissitudes of the Sarmatian Stereotype"], in *Studia Romantyczne*, ed. Maria Żmigrodzka (Wrocław: Zakład Narodowy im. Ossolińskich, 1973), p. 246
16 Manfred Kridl, *Antagonizm wieszczòw* [The Antagonism of the Bards] (Warszawa: Wydawnictwo Arcta, 1925), pp. 178–172. Turowski points out that in ending his play with the complete annihilation of the Weneds, instead of a mingling of the tribes, Słowacki departs from contemporary historians' accounts of the origins of Poland.

Greek motif with the Polish. Słowacki in several works alludes to Homer's "harp," but the instrument has particular thematic significance in *Lilla Weneda*, where the harpists, the national bards, carry the proto-Polish national identity. According to Juliusz Kleiner, Słowacki's use of the harp in this Greek setting, in particular in a text that was published with *Lilla Weneda*, reinforces the identification of Greece with Poland.[17]

[3]
Here among the stones busy Arachne
Quarrels with the breeze, which tears her yarn.
Here the fragrance of sad savory drifts over scorched mountains,
Here the wind, whipping through the grey piles of ruins,
Drives flower seeds on – and the down
Wanders and flits around the tomb like spirits,

[4]
Here field crickets among the stones,
Hiding from the sun that shines above the tomb,
Hiss as if they wished to silence me.
This hissing that one hears in tombs
Is a terrifying coda to a song –
It is a revelation, a hymn, a psalm of silence.

[5]
I am quiet like you, o Atreides!
Whose ashes sleep beneath the watchful crickets.
Neither am I ashamed of my insignificance
Nor do my thoughts soar like eagles.
I am deeply humble and calm here,
In this tomb of fame, crime, pride.

---

17   J. Kleiner, *Juljusz Słowacki,* vol. 2, pp. 253ff.

[6]
A young oak shoots up in the stone triangle
On the carved granite over the door to the tomb.
It was planted by sparrows, or maybe pigeons,
And blooms black leaves that do not allow
The sun to enter the dark tomb;
I plucked one leaf from the black bush;

[7]
No spirit or ghost wrested it from me,
Nor did a specter groan in the branches;
Only the shaft of sunlight grew bigger,
And golden light spilled at my feet.
I thought at once that this brightness breaking in
Was a string from Homer's harp;

In stanzas 3 and 4 the natural denizens of this abandoned site – spiders and crickets – create a link between Antiquity and the poet. The wind in stanza 3 picks up from the image of stanza 2, the wind bearing (becoming) Electra's voice. In stanza 3 it carries downy seeds (implying fruitfulness) that are like spirits. The wind (inspiration) destroys the spider webs and scatters plant seeds. The spider is linked to ancient Greece – he calls it Arachne, evoking the mythological story of the spinner who was punished by a jealous Athena. Also, the crickets are Słowacki's fellow bards – hissing the poet to silence, their quiet itself a form of music, religious or spiritual ("rhapsody," "hymn").

The crickets have a resonance here with Plato's *Phaedrus*. In this dialogue the philosopher Socrates tells Phaedrus that crickets, or cicadas, are connected to the muses:

> The story is that once upon a time these creatures were men – men of an age before there were any muses – and that when the latter came into the world, and music made

its appearance, some of the people of those days were so thrilled with pleasure that they went on singing, and quite forgot to eat and drink until they actually died without noticing it. From them in due course sprang the race of cicadas, to which the Muses have granted the boon of needing no sustenance right from their birth, but of singing from the very first, without food or drink, until the day of their death, after which they go and report to the Muses how they severally are paid honor among mankind, and by whom. (259: b–c)[18]

Socrates' point is that they must continue talking and *avoid sleep* to gain the respect of the crickets, whose "siren song" is intended to lull men to sleep: "There is every reason for us not to yield to slumber in the noontide, but to pursue our talk" (259: d).[19]

Słowacki's poet resists the sleep of the early stanzas and sits quietly, in expectation, as indicated in the following stanza (5). In stanzas 6 and 7 he takes a bold step: he invades the tomb by plucking the blocking oak leaf, allowing in the sun, which he takes to be a harp string and then he awakens, as if realizing none of it was real. The dramatic change in tone at the end of stanza 9, achieved by the call "to horse!" ("Na koń!"), indicates a sudden emotional upsurge, as well as a thematic change of pace. It is as though the poet, following Socrates' suggestion, shakes himself awake and leaves the tomb and its drowsy emptiness, and goes on with his journey. Now he must decide where to stop to contemplate Poland's history: he has confronted the theme of crime (Electra, Orestes, Agamemnon); he has

18 Plato, *Phaedrus*, translated by R. Hackforth, in Plato's *Collected Dialogues*, ed. Edith Hamilton and Huntington Cairns (Princeton: Princeton University Press, 1989).

19 Słowacki's knowledge of Plato's dialogue *Phaedrus*, and *Symposium* and *Phaedo* as well, is attested by numerous allusions in *Kordian*. See T. Sinko, *Hellenizm Juliusza Słowackiego*, p. 73.

failed to revive the far-off golden harp of Homer, and must find a place that fits the song about Poland.

The thematic tapestry of the nine opening stanzas introduces the main elements of Antiquity – Electra, Orestes and Aeneas – used by Słowacki to explore the fate of Poland. The poet responds to the admonition of the crickets by approaching the tomb and its denizens with religious humility, eschewing individual traits of pride and shame for the crime. Yet, he is "like" the Atreides (as Electra's voice echoed his own in stanza 2, and since his heart sleeps in stanza 1 like their dust sleeps in the tomb). He says he is "quiet like you," as if his silence can be identified with death.

The invocation of the voice coming from the leaf can also be found in the *Aeneid*, and this allusion brings to mind the Trojans who suffered and lost their country. Aeneas, the Trojan prince who survived the destruction of his homeland, sets out for a new homeland, to resurrect Troy elsewhere. The Roman poet Virgil – to whom Słowacki pays homage at the beginning of his *Voyage to the Holy Land* – sings of Aeneas' wanderings and the founding myth of the origin of Rome. Słowacki links these two sets of allusions: the image of the tomb as a guarded place continues in stanza 7, and the visit to a grave is like the poet's entrance to the underworld. In the opening stanzas, the sun and the outside world are still present but remote: the far-off "golden harp" (stanza 2), the scent of thyme that smells of the "scorched mountains" (outside the tomb), and the crickets that are "hiding from the sun above the tomb" (also outside). In stanza 6 the small tree, planted by birds, "protects" the entrance from the intruding light of the sun (fear of intrusion is expressed clearly: the leaves "do not allow" or "let in" the light: *nie puszcza*). The poet tests the strength of the guardians by picking a single leaf. The incident recalls Aeneas' passage into the underworld in Virgil's *Aeneid*, Book VI – where the golden bough allows safe passage to the realm of spirits.

Graves are protected by spirits in Virgil and their consent allows a confrontation with the past; Aeneas' visit to the underworld allows a prophecy for the future of Rome. He finds out about the past and hears about the future. The hints of the *Aeneid* in *Agamemnon's Tomb* are more evocations than allusions, but the significance of Virgil would not have been lost on Słowacki's readers, who would be aware of the patriotic allegory the story had for Poland in the post-partition period, where the image of Aeneas came to represent the Polish national identity.[20] Given the familiarity of the connections, Słowacki's visit to the tomb becomes part of a larger quest for a vision of his own country's freedom, following the model of Aeneas: just as Aeneas is allowed to visit the underworld to find out from his father's ghost the glorious vision of Troy's future in Rome, similarly, the reader expects, Słowacki will summon his father's spirit to see Poland's future. And, indeed, the bulk of the poem is a discussion of Poland's past and future. In fact the poet's fathers (his real father and his poetic fathers) do appear at the close of the poem.

However, Słowacki seems to treat this trope (Aeneas in the underworld) ironically from the very beginning. His entrance to the tomb has a somewhat mocking tone. Also, the rejection of the elaborate elegiac setup in stanza 9, where, "full of disgust," he will abandon the tomb to find his inspiration elsewhere, is consistent with the way he debunks the familiar tropes of romantic poetics and political ideas throughout the *Voyage* and his later work, *Beniowski*. For example, his plucking the leaf is

20 See Leon T. Błaszczyk, "The Mickiewicz Generation and the Classical Heritage: A Contribution to the Study of Polish Neo-Humanism," in Victor Terras, ed., *American Contributions to the Eighth International Congress of Slavists. Zagreb and Ljubljana, September 3–9, 1978*. Vol. 2. Literature, (Columbus, OH: Slavica, 1978), pp. 48–81: "Troy symbolized Poland which one day would be resurrected to a new, more magnificent life" (p. 68).

described in terms of an "attack" that goes unchallenged ("Nie bronił mi go żaden duch" – literally, "no spirit defended it from me"). As in Aeneas's case, the bough allows him access to the underworld, and for this reason critics read the passage in Słowacki as a simple bestowal of "consent" to enter on the part of the tombs' guardians (the crickets, the spirits).[21] However, Słowacki uses an image of desecration to describe the ray of sunlight he has let in or summoned, as it falls to his feet: the light "intrudes" or "breaks into" the tomb (the Polish "wbiegło" suggests this, "spilled in," "ran inside"). The very phrase "fell to my feet" ("i do nóg mi padło") suggests the poet's triumph or conquest over the divinity he expects to protect the tomb. Throughout stanza 7 the language of intrusion seems to undermine the idea of permission: instead the emptiness, the absence of spirits, is emphasized in this passage.

[8]
And I stretched my hand out in the darkness,
To tune it and pluck it and, trembling,
Force it to tears and to song – and to anger
At the great nothingness of graves and this silent
Handful of dust. But in my hand
This string trembled and vanished without complaint.

[9]
And so – it is my fate to sit on tombstones
And seek out insignificant, frail sorrows.
It is my fate to rule over sleepy kingdoms,
To have mute harps and deaf listeners.

---

21 See, for example, Ryszard Przybylski, *Podróż Juliusza Słowackiego na Wschód* [Juliusz Słowacki's Voyage to the East] (Kraków: Wydawnictwo Literackie, 1982), p. 29. Sinko, *Hellenizm Juliusza Słowackiego*, p. 113.

Or dead ones. And so, full of disgust . . .
To horse! I want sun, wind, the sound of hoof beats!

[10]
To horse!... Here, along the bed of a dry stream,
Where pink laurel blossoms flow instead of water,
As if a shining storm were chasing me,
I fly with tears and with intense, flashing eyes,
And my horse's legs stretch on the wind.
If he stumbles over a grave where knights rest – he'll fall.

These three stanzas mark the change, the transition to the core of *Agamemnon's Tomb*: first evoking a link between Poland and Greece, and then changing to criticism of Poland. The tone here is not of genuine pathos but of irony. Słowacki rejects what is expected of him. The loaded word "disgust" anticipates the theme of "shame" that later characterizes the feeling Poles should have about the failed uprising. No one could call the sorrows sung by Homer or Sophocles "trivial, flimsy, frail," but they could seem trivial if in a time of national crisis focusing on ancient history and, in particular, art, seems unimportant.[22] Like Alphonse de Lamartine in "La liberté. Ou une nuit à Rome," Słowacki mocks the romantic trope of seeking a "haunted ruin" for inspiration and ruminations on national contemporary history vis-à-vis Antiquity. (Byron as well follows this poetic pattern in *Childe Harold's Pilgrimage*.)

The horse is the poet's creative fancy, the vehicle for his metaphoric transport, like the frantic horse rides in such familiar works as *Childe Harold's Pilgrimage* ("To horse! To horse! he quits, for ever quits/ a scene of peace though soothing to his soul,"

---

22 Compare Anna Akhmatova's comments on the horrors of 20th century Russian history: "Shakespeare's plays–the sensational atrocities, passions, duels–are child's play compared to the life of each one of us."

I: 28), and Mickiewicz's *Crimean Sonnets* (sonnet 10, "Bajdary": "I release my horse to the wind and spare not the crop" ["Wypuszczam na wiatr konia i nie szczędzę razów"]). The image of the flying horse signals a change in perspective: from the literal site of Agamemnon's tomb in the first stanzas, which recalled the memory of ancient events, to more recent events in Polish history in the next stanzas.[23] The flying horse is the poet's mind, ranging over the landmarks of the history of Poland. The horse must stop to point out the relationship between Poland and Greece.

23   Przybylski associates the horse with the symbol of "unbridled" passions, a "panic-stricken" emotional state, and the world of dreams, as found in the Platonic dialogue *Phaedrus* – the same dialogue alluded to in the poem in the stanzas describing the cicadas – and the frothing horses associated with nightmares in the paintings of Fuseli, Delacroix and Stubbs. There are a number of problems with Przybylski's suggestion. First of all, in *Agamemnon's Tomb* the departure from the tomb is not inspired by fear, but only disgust. Second, the poet is not being controlled by the horse, but summons it ("Na koń!"), and his stated destination is the place the horse will decide to stop (stumble).

If the image of the horse has any artistic source, Słowacki could have borrowed it from the British poets. In "O Poezjach Bohdana Zaleskiego" ("On Bohdan Zaleski's Poetry"; in *Dzieła* [*Works*], XI, p. 146) Słowacki quotes Byron's comment about Southey: "Even Wordsworth has frequent flights of fancy and when he demands a flight to the heavens . . . at one point he even cries out: "O a boat! A boat! So that I could sail across the expanse of the heavens!" Byron laughed at this," writes Słowacki, "saying that that man should have mounted not a boat but a hot-air balloon, or mounted Southey's Pegasus . . . and I [Słowacki] think only in the greatest efforts of might and spirit could one ask a miracle of God." Byron's satire of Wordsworth, Coleridge and Southey occurs in *English Bards and Scotch Reviewers*; toward the end of the poem he writes of Pegasus: "Ye! Who in Granta's honours would surpass,/ Must mount her Pegasus, a full-grown ass" (ll. 969–970). The Wordsworth lines Słowacki alludes to here are, most probably, from the prologue to *Peter Bell*: "There's something in a flying horse,/ There's something in a huge balloon;/But through the clouds I'll never float/ Until I have a little Boat"; etc. The ship and horse equivalence in Coleridge occurs in *The Rime of the Ancient Mariner*.

Part 3.

Poland and Greece:

"Thermopylae? No, Chaeronea."

[11]
At Thermopylae? – No, at Chaeronea –
That is where my horse must stop.
For I am from a land where the specter of hope
Is like a dream for hearts of little faith.
For if my horse is frightened in his flight,
Then that grave is equal to – ours.

[12]
A legion of dead Spartans is ready
To chase me from the grave at Thermopylae,
For I am from the sad land of Ilots,
From a land where despair does not rain down on graves,
From a land where after unhappy days
There always remains a sad half of knights alive.

This strange concluding line, about knights who are ambiguously either "half alive" or "half knights," characterizes Poland as opposed to Sparta (not necessarily Greece). Calling Poland a land of "Ilots," a word presumably meant to evoke the Spartan slave caste of "helots," Słowacki alludes to the foreign partitions that subjugated Poland during the previous century. This is another way *Agamemnon's Tomb* connects with *Lilla Weneda*, whose hero, Wened, a prototype for the Polish nobleman, draws on the motif of the "half-knight." As Sinko writes, Wened is "a half-knight who lived after the death of Lelum": "he does not risk death himself."[1] Słowacki at first intended *Agamemnon's Tomb* to be the prologue, not the epilogue, to *Lilla Weneda*, in which case the link between Greece and Polish history would have been even more overt.

The characterization of Poland as a "land where despair builds no memorials to fame" ("Z kraju – gdzie rozpacz nie sypie kurhanów") in the second stanza is equally baffling. Kleiner glosses it in the following way: "a land where people do not die from despair but even after disaster are able to be reconciled with life."[2] This capacity for "life goes on" should not necessarily be a negative trait, but it is evoked here in a context where it is surely meant to be critical, in a passage explaining the incongruity between Spartans and Poles. It suggests here compromise ("half alive") and passive resignation. Moreover, it points to the original structure Słowacki intended for the poem before publishing it with *Lilla Weneda* and ending

1   Sinko, *Hellenizm Juliusza Słowackiego*, p. 112. The half-knights are evoked likewise in the figure of Polelum in *Lilla Weneda* (his name suggests "pol," or "half," as well as "po," or "after"). Also, see Libera: "A shameful, incomplete, half-lethargic heroism [of the fighters in the November Uprising] became defined as a national blemish in the epithet 'sad half-knights.' This sounds like an echo of the sleeping knights, also contained in the basic ideas of *Kordian* and *Horsztyński* [. . .] This legend was known for a long time in Poland: 'In a certain city, in a mountain cave, knights sleep [. . .] they will awaken when war breaks out over faith or freedom.'"

For the structure of *Agyzelausz*, based on Plutarch's lives of the Spartan kings Agis and Cleomenes, see Sinko, *Hellada i Roma w Polsce* [Hellada and Roma in Poland] (Lwów: Państwowe wydawnictwo książek szkolnych, 1933), pp. 16–19.

2   *Lilla Weneda i Grób Agamemnona*, p. 179.

it after stanza 21. Canto 8 of *Voyage to the Holy Land* ends with a strange and homey image of sparrows in a description of the typical Polish landscape. This odd line here anticipates the return to this theme in the original form of the poem, which ended with a rejection of high Romantic aesthetics ("Bloody volcano"): "For you are mocked by the sparrows' chirping/ And the early morning crowing of morning roosters."

[13]
At Thermopylae I do not dare
To lead my horse through the pass;
For there must be such faces there, whose gaze
Would crush the heart of every Pole for shame.
I will not stand there before the spirit of Greece –
No, I would die first rather than go there in chains.

[14]
At Thermopylae – what would I say
If the knights rose before me on their grave,
And, showing me their bloodied chests,
Asked me plainly: "Were there many of you?
Forget the distance of long centuries between us."
If they asked me this – what would I say?

[15]
At Thermopylae a body lies
Without red cloak or golden sash.
It is the naked corpse of Leonidas:
A beautiful soul dwells in its marble form.
For a long time the people mourned his sacrifice,
The scented flame and broken goblet.

The poet is trying to find a resting place for his horse at the Greek grave that would be a counterpart of the Polish one, but he says in stanza 11 that the grave that meets such a condition is Chaerona (the site of a battle in 338BC), not Thermopylae.

Słowacki then elaborates (in stanzas 12 and 13) that he could not face the accusing ghosts of the Spartans at Thermopylae. However, in stanza 14 he introduces the naked, unadorned corpse of Leonidas, which then prompts his consideration of Poland's history in the following section. In other words, after declaring that Thermopylae is not the place to compare with Poland, he proceeds strangely to base his contrast on Thermopylae, never mentioning Chaeronea again.

The context of Polish historical events here is the failed November Uprising of 1830–1831. Its failure was naturally the subject of heated debates in Polish society and mutual accusations which led to various evaluations of the causes of the failure. Słowacki's stanzas can be read as the poet's voice in, or an echo of, these debates. At first glance the imagined question posed by the imagined Spartans – "Were there many of you?" – seems to mean Słowacki is repeating the claim that the uprising failed, like Thermopylae, because the Poles were outnumbered. However, the argument proceeds in a more intricate manner.

The analogy between Thermopylae and the November Uprising turns on possible explanations for the defeat of Poland. Thermopylae is the pass that 300 Spartans defended and where they all died. These Spartans and their leader, King Leonidas, became an emblem of heroism, preferring glorious death to survival. Thermopylae was followed by the victory of the pan-Hellenic forces over the Persians at Salamis a year later. This was the first time Greeks feel a pan-Hellenic bond or a sense of "national" unity, as can be gathered from Herodotus' *Histories* and Aeschylus' play *The Persians*. Comparing the November Uprising to Thermopylae implies that its failure could be explained by overwhelming odds. The defeat of the 300 Spartans at Thermopylae, which allowed the

Greeks to organize themselves before Salamis, suggests that the deaths of the Spartans served a greater purpose. The question of numbers comes up in both Aeschylus and Herodotus – how could the Greeks at Salamis defeat the vast armies of the Persians? – and is given two explanations. The distraught Persian Queen Atossa in Aeschylus' play asks the messenger:

How great was the number of the ships of Hellas. . .?

Messenger:
Were numbers all, be well assured the barbarians would have gained the victory with their fleet.[. . .] Think'st thou we were outnumbered in this contest? No, it was some power divine that swayed down the scale of fortune with unequal weight and thus destroyed our host.[3]

One may read Aeschylus' words as attributing the Greek victory to some divine intervention or providential force; however, a less poetic account in the historian Herodotus supplements Aeschylus' account. The victory was due to the Greeks' strategic genius, their organization, and their ability to leave internal quarrels aside. To quote Herodotus: "The Athenians waived their claim" to command of the Greek forces "in the interest of national survival, knowing that a quarrel about the command would certainly mean the destruction of Greece."[4]

Chaeronea, on the other hand, evokes a symbolic layer of the end of an independent nation, and thus invites parallels with an earlier defeat in Polish history, that of the Kościuszko

---

3   Aeschylus, *The Persians*, ll. 331–346, translated by Herbert Weir Smyth, in *Aeschylus*, 2 vols. (London/Cambridge, Massachusetts: William Heineman/Harvard University Press, 1973), vol. 1, p. 139.

4   Herodotus, *The Histories*, translated by Aubrey de Selincourt (London: Penguin Classics, 1971), Bk. IX, p. 499.

Insurrection in 1794, and the defeat at Maciejowice that was
followed by the last partition of Poland in 1795. For this reason
Maciejowice could be seen as a counterpart to Chaeronea,
which marked the final defeat of free Greek cities by the army
of Philip of Macedon (father of Alexander the Great). The
infighting and disorganization among the Greeks and their lack
of "national" unity allowed Philip to win. The battle of
Chaeronea went down in legend as the moment glorious Greece
lost its independence forever. Although the analogy is not overt
in *Agamemnon's Tomb*, Słowacki equates Maciejowice with
Chaeronea earlier in the *Voyage to the Holy Land*, Canto 4.
Since none of the other cantos in *Voyage* has been translated
into English, we quote the stanzas here at some length:

[41]
All of them – except the leader . . . he will not rise,
Killed by the sword of a fallen state,
But other spirits in an urn-like vase
Are buried in the breast of a marble lion.
This was their monument after death,
They have left – and the monument has been shattered to
pieces.

[42]
The spirits smashed the lion's growing breast!
Today it lies on a lonely plain
Like crossbows blown up by gunpowder,
But the head full of eternal pain
Has fallen on the ground – it seems as if asleep,
Sad and terrible in its expired soul.

[43]
For a long time did the Greek look at this lion's head
As on one fallen silent from misfortune;

The sculptor gave the marble a sad eloquence.
While gazing – I heard Kościuszko's two words:
"Finis Poloniae," preserved in the stone
Like a tear in a rock – or thought in a picture.

[44]
O Chaeronea! O Maciejowice!
Hush! . . . Something white shines in the foliage . . .
Ah, no! it is only some white doves
That flew through the garden walk . . .
Come again, my book, thrown on the flowers,
I will read again – it is not yet she.

[45]
Money clinks – the Greek tosses on the scale
A diamond sheath of his sword;
Not enough yet . . . he threw in the steel blade,
Pay with iron . . . Suddenly Pasha Ibrahim,
Like the Nile that flows into all waters of the world,
Or like the pyramid crumbling from on high,

[46]
Falls upon Greece – where is Thermopylae,
Through which Xerxes's serpent crawled before,
Where are these men who did not tremble
At the moment of death – and died?... Tsavellas
On the fields of Klisova with 800 men
Blocked the way to two Pashas – and waits.[5]

5 Słowacki is alluding in this stanza to the fall of Missolonghi during the
Greek Uprising of 1826. Ibrahim Pasha was one of the two main leaders
of the Turks, along with Reshid Pasha ("two Pashas"). Kitsos Tsevellas
was the general in charge of defense of the island of Klisova, a strategic
fort in the lagoon off Missolonghi during the siege. See David Brewer,
The Greek War of Independence. The Struggle for Freedom from

[47]
I hear my heart beating in my breast,
It seems as if I'm looking at Leonidas' corpse,
Looking deeply – I wait for him to come to life –
And at that moment the beauty of the bright flowers,
And the dove flying through the garden
Disappeared from my eyes.[6]

Kościuszko's Insurrection is important for other reasons: Kościuszko included peasantry into his forces. Unable to provide proper military weapons for all, he armed peasants with weapons made out of scythes (the so-called scythe-bearers, *kosynierzy*). Kościuszko also understood that without social reforms, the peasantry cannot have a patriotic interest in the fight for independence. All men who defend their country should be free. As Thomas Jefferson described Kościuszko: "He is the most noble son of Liberty I have ever known; the Liberty for all, not just for rich or few."[7] During the Insurrection, on May 7, 1794, Kościuszko issued the proclamation known as the "Połaniec Proclamation" (named for the

Ottoman Oppression and the Birth of the Modern Greek Nation (Woodstock and New York: The Overlook Press, 2001), pp. 278–286.

6   Striking echoes of imagery from *Agamemon's Tomb* and Canto 8 are apparent in this fragment: the soul trapped in marble, a white vision glimpsed in the foliage, etc. These stanzas merit more systematic poetic study than we have room for in this work.

7   Quoted in Maria Janion and Maria Żmigrodzka, *Romantyzm i historia* [Romanticism and History] (Gdańsk: Słowo/Obraz Terytoria, 2001), pp. 285–286. Kościuszko's correspondence provides evidence that he was deeply moved by the condition of slaves in America. Although their living conditions were, as he writes, incomparably worse than those of the Polish peasantry, it is very likely that this American experience lies at the root of his social reforms in Poland. After the American Revolution, Kościuszko wanted to have his estate in America sold and the profits go toward buying out American slaves and granting them freedom.

place where it was announced), promising to arrange the "feudal obligations of the peasants" and secure for them "effective governmental protection, safety of property, and justice." According to radical reformers, such as Maurycy Mochnacki, Kościuszko did not go far enough and therefore Poland lost because of him.[8] Because the inclusion of the peasantry was not repeated in the later uprising of 1830, some Słowacki scholars read the question "Were there many of you?" as referring to the absence of the peasantry in the Uprising, and, implicitly, as Słowacki's criticism of the social stratification of the Polish nation. Słowacki's numerous references to Mochnacki, particularly in *Beniowski* and in the *Voyage*, have naturally led readers to the conclusion that Słowacki shared Mochnacki's reformist ideas. But the degree of Słowacki's commitment in 1839 will forever remain a matter of speculation.

In fact, it was a widespread view that the uprising failed because of the overwhelming numerical superiority of the Russians over the Poles, and the comparison with Thermopylae was regularly made in the émigré community.

8   One should point out that, according to Maurycy Mochnacki, Władyslaw Heltman, a radical democrat and the author of a revisionist article about Kościuszko, "Półśrodki" ("Half-means"), accused Kościuszko of being guilty of the failed insurrection. Kościuszko, a man of great integrity, Heltman claimed, did not carry social reforms far enough to have secured the success of the Insurrection. In summarizing Heltman's view (in which he followed Mochnacki), Janion and Żmigrodzka write in their massive study of Polish Romanticism: "It is true that it was the gentry's egoism that caused Poland's death, but Kościuszko is guilty in that, though he had the power, he did not take advantage of the 'radical means' that were necessary at the moment." *Ibid.*, p. 287. On the attitude toward the peasantry in Polish revolutionary discourse in this period, see Brian Porter, *When Nationalism Began to Hate: Imagining Modern Politics in Nineteenth-Century Poland* (Oxford: Oxford UP, 2000), especially the section on "The Revolutionary Nation," pp. 28–36.

According to Leszek Libera, "the concept of this stanza [stanza 14] seems to have its origin in the reading of Maurycy Mochnacki's *Powstanie narodu polskiego w r. 1830 i 1831 (The Insurrection of the Polish Nation in the years 1830 and 1831)*."[9] Mochnacki was a publicist, a literary critic, émigré political activist, and a participant in the Uprising. His book, written immediately after the events of 1831, set parameters for the émigré debates about the chances of the Uprising. Not surprisingly, many of Mochnacki's points seem to have found their way to *Agamemnon's Tomb*: the debate over the failure of the Uprising because of numbers, which may implicitly suggest, particularly if one remembers Kościuszko's use of the scythe-bearer units, the lack of the peasantry's involvement, and, finally, the critical account of the privileges of the Polish nobility. It is worth discussing Mochnacki's ideas in some detail.

If one of the reasons for the success of the Greeks against the Persians at Salamis was their strategic genius and organization, the opposite could be said of the Poles in 1830.[10] "In the common view among the émigrés, the reason for the failure of the November uprising was an objective fact": in the question "Were there many of you?" Leszek Libera relates, Polish Conservatives "pointed out the source of failure," that is, the numeric superiority of the enemy. And, Libera continues, "European opinion" supported this reading, which Mochnacki refers to by saying: "According to them [Europeans] we were just a handful of brave men, and the enemy was a giant. They

---

9   Leszek Libera, *Juliusza Słowackiego "Podróż" do Ziemi Świętej z Neapolu"* [Juliusz Słowacki's *Voyage to the Holy Land from Naples*] (Poznań: Pro Scientia, 1999), p. 103.

10 Norman Davies, in *God's Playground. A History of Poland, 1795 to the Present*, Vol. II (Oxford: Oxford UP, 1981), writes of the "ineptitude" of the leaders of the Uprising and the "violence and confusion [that] erupted on the night of 28 November" (pp. 317–318).

imagine our last insurrection as a battle of the small David with the enormous Goliath."[11] Mochnacki's goal in his *Insurrection of the Polish Nation* is to demonstrate that "the revolution of November 29th could have succeeded."[12] "We were not just a *few* [*garstka*; Mochnacki's italics] at the beginning. We became this only later, because of the erroneous direction of the whole uprising. It is better to admit this mistake, it is better to point it out, it is better to summon before the judgment of history those who are responsible, rather than judge the whole nation as deprived of reason, so that one can justify the future shortcomings of political and military leaders;"[13] and: "I repeat, never has Poland been more powerful."[14] In other words, the November Uprising failed not because of the numerical superiority of the enemies' forces but because of the military and organizational mismanagement of Polish resources.[15] As if recalling the

11   Libera, *Podróż Juliusza Słowackiego*, p. 104. Libera's analysis leaves room for some queries: It is uncertain whether the opinion about the battle of Goliath and David is that of the "Europeans." Mochnacki's actual sentence preceding the quotation reads "There are people among us" who say that "Poles, people of hot temperament, never think before they act. They assess neither their own strength, nor that of the enemy, and merely follow the voice of honor, conscience and obligation, and set out to fight." The introductory clause, "There are people among us . . ." seems to refer to the opinion of some Polish émigré figures rather than to that of the Europeans. In which case, the quoted opinion is an exercise in "national self-criticism."

12   Mochnacki, *Powstanie*, vol. 1, pp. 34–35.

13   Mochnacki, *ibid.*, vol. 1, p. 35. Note that the word "garstka" (a few, or a "handful") is used by Słowacki in *Agamemnon's Tomb*, in stanza 8: "the great nothingness of graves and silent handful of dust [*garstka popiołu*]."

14   *Ibid.*,vol. 1, p. 31.

15   *Ibid.*, vol 1, p. 71. Mochnacki here demonstrates the widespread support for the November 29th revolution: "The peasants and noblemen, old and young, even children, cripples, all of them were ready to be enlisted . . .

inscription on the Spartan tomb, Mochnacki states: "How painful, how shameful are these truths! [One could only wish that] the future generations can read on our graves: we lost our lives, not because of lack of strength, but [rather], because we could not use it well."[16] Unlike the Spartan self-sacrifice at Thermopylae, which allowed the Greeks to slow the progress of the Persian army and gather the pan-Hellenic forces before the victorious battle of Salamis, the Poles passed up the opportunity offered by the situation in 1830. As Libera points out, Mochnacki's book provided Słowacki with a "ready-made moral and poetic formula for his judgment of the November generation."[17] He continues:

> Mochnacki quoted the speech by Piotr Wysocki, who opened up his famous chapter of the history of Poland with a parallel with Thermopylae: Poles! The hour of vengeance has struck! Today we will win or we will die. Show our enemies our chests so that they become their Thermopylae.[18]

According to Mochnacki, the fight for independence must include peasantry.[19] For this, however, one needed a

---

This mass, so enthusiastic, one could easily organize at a given time. . . . There were some thirty thousand Polish troops."

16   *Ibid.*, vol. 2, p. 580. The inscription over the graves at Thermopylae reads: "Go, stranger, and tell the Spartans that we lie here in obedience to their laws."

17   Libera, *Juliusza Słowackiego Podróż*, p. 104.

18   Mochnacki, *Powstanie*, vol. 2, p. 13. (See Libera, *ibid.*, p. 104).

19   Mochnacki, *Powstanie*, vol. 1, p. 33: "The war with foreign oppressors needs great strength; this strength lives in the mass of the nation, in the greater part of it, which only in one part of the country (in the Congress Kingdom) has the same privileges before the law as the nobility, and in all other provinces it finds itself in a state of ignorance, and the horrible [. . .] state of slavery and without any share in property. To get this majority interested, to awaken it to the fight against a foreign enemy [. . .] to change it and make its civic and property conditions better is the revolutionary part, the social part of the Polish uprisings."

clear plan of social reforms: the (partial) abolition of serf-dom, the right to vote, and equality before the law. Needless to say, such reforms would inevitably require changing the privileges of the Polish nobility.[20] Read through the prism of Mochnacki's book, Słowacki's "Were there many of you?" acquires a different shade. The answer might be: "No, there were not enough of us. We failed because only part of the Polish nation took part in the battle of 'Thermopylae'." That is: the peasantry did not join. This "democratic" message remains the bone of contention in Słowacki scholarship.

Słowacki's lines about the dead Spartans do not end on the question: "Were there many of you?" He continues: "forget that long centuries have passed" ("Zapomnij, że jest długi wieków przedział").[21] Słowacki is possibly following Byron,

20   Mochnacki saw the problem with Polish nobility very clearly. As long as things worked in their favor they did not care about social reforms too much. After the partition of Poland and before the ascension to the throne by Nicholas I, the Polish nobility "enjoyed privileges that made them have little interest in the fight for independence." "The nobleman did not pay any taxes, he was not conscripted, the peasant carried all financial burdens. In such a state of affairs, the nobleman enjoyed freedoms under the Muscovite rule that did not make him think of a unified, independent and particularly free Poland. What else could he hope for? Wasn't he a king – more than a constitutional king – in his own village? After the death of Alexander I, the Muscovite government abandoned such politics [that favored the Polish nobility]." *Ibid.*, vol. 1, p. 37.

   Mochnacki's ideas were borne out by later events: "In the end," writes Norman Davies, "to drive a wedge between the Polish peasant and the incorrigible Polish nobility, the Tsar was obliged in the decree of April 1864 to grant Emancipation on more favorable terms than in any other part of the Empire." *Heart of Europe. A Short History of Poland* (Oxford: Oxford University Press, 1986), p. 168.

21   It is not clear in the manuscript where the quotation marks were supposed to end the quotation. However, this is the most logical variant. See the editors' note in Krzyżanowski's edition of Słowacki, *Dzieła* [*Works*], vol. IV, p. 313.

who evokes the spirit of the Ancients to inspire modern Greece in *Childe Harold* canto 2:

When riseth Lacedemon's hardihood
[. . . .]
When Grecian mothers shall give birth to men
Then may'st thou be restored; but not till then.

And Byron strikes his final note, which sounds reminiscent of Słowacki's line "forget that long centuries have passed":

Can man its shatter'd splendour renovate.
Recall its virtues back, and vanquish Time and Fate?
(LXXXIV)

Let us emphasize: whatever the reason for the failure of the Uprising, lack of courage was not one of them, and the Poles could hardly feel shamed by the Spartans in this respect. True, Słowacki writes: "I will not stand there before the spirit of Greece – / No, I would die first rather than go there – in chains." However, it is unreasonable to think that Słowacki is calling for the collective suicide of a nation, a sort of Polish Masada, to avoid the fate of becoming a race of helots.[22]
    As Herodotus informs us:

22   "Słowacki interpreted the death of the Spartans in Thermopylae as a conscious flight from slavery into death. According to him, Thermopylae was the work of heroic souls, who prefer death to humiliation." R. Przybylski, *Podróż Juliusza Słowackiego na Wschód* (pp. 31–32). See also T. Sinko, *Hellada i Roma w Polsce* [*Hellas and Roma in Poland*] (pp. 15–16): "From the grave of the Spartans in Thermopylae he, being a Pole, who comes from the country of the Ilots (helots, slaves), was chased away by the ghosts of the dead, because they could not die like the Spartans, to the very last man. Those ghosts/spirits [of the Spartans] would ask him: 'How many of you were there (in the insurrection)?' And he [Słowacki] would have to be silent."

> [R]ight at the outset of the war the Spartans had been told
> by the oracle, when they asked for advice, that either their
> city must be laid waste by the foreigner or one of their kings
> be killed . . . I believe it was the thought of this oracle, com-
> bined with his wish to lay up for the Spartans a treasure of
> fame in which no other city should share, that made
> Leonidas dismiss those troops [. . .] And indeed by remain-
> ing at his post he left a great name behind him [. . .][23]

The death of the 300 Spartans was a trade-off, so to speak. The
300 died so that Sparta (and Greece) could live. However glo-
rious was Leonidas' fight, he knew from prophesy that his
death was the price he needed to pay for Sparta's freedom. The
question is not, as is usually suggested, about becoming helots
or not, but whether the sacrifice was worth it. The Spartan sac-
rifice was worth it because the Greeks ultimately triumphed; in
the case of Poland, on the other hand, Poles lost both their lives
and the chance to be a free nation again.

As mentioned above, it is likely that in these and the next
few stanzas Słowacki was inspired by Byron's *Childe Harold*
canto II, where the poet explains to the Greeks that foreign
powers will not free them:

Will Gaul or Muscovite redress ye? No!
True, they may lay your proud despoilers low.
But not for you will Freedom's altars Flame.
Shades of the Helots! Triumph o'er your foe!
Greece! Change thy lords, thy state is still the same;
Thy glorious day is o'er, but not thy years of shame.
(LXXVI)

Because of the strong parallels with Polish history, or the psy-
chology of it, the lines written by the English poet would strike

---

23   Herodotus, *Histories*, Book VII, p. 491.

a familiar chord in every Polish reader, let alone a Polish poet who tried to read as much of modern Greek history as his own; more so even than modern Greeks in Słowacki's time, Poles were expected to choose culturally and politically between "Gaul" (the French) and "Muscovite" (the Russians). It looks like Byron's "satellite," as Sinko calls Słowacki, "rehearsed" some parts of Byron's message in Polish. Like the modern Greeks called by Byron "Shades of the Helots," Poles are compared to the helots by Słowacki; like theirs, the glory of Poland is gone, and, again, no one except Poles can help Poland become free.

Not unlike Byron, who puts Greeks to shame by comparing them to helots with sickles who have forgotten their ancient heritage,[24] Słowacki too makes the Polish nation "stand ashamed" before the spirit of Greece. However, the parallel has a limited application. The Polish fighters demonstrated as much military valor, during both the Kościuszko Insurrection and the November Uprising, as the ancient Greek warriors. What the Poles can be faulted on, however, was their lack of the one thing that in Mochnacki's view would have made it possible for them to regain their independence: strategic planning on the one hand and, on the other, political unity.

Słowacki wrote and delivered his poem nine years after the November Uprising – that is, at a time when the nation must have been psychologically devastated. If the poem is not merely an assessment of the past, but an assessment of its future chances (this is suggested by its continuation in "Wschód

---

24 This disparaging view of contemporary Greeks is exemplified in Chateaubriand: "though he expressed some sympathy for the modern Greeks, he denied them any affinity with their classical progenitors." Olga Augustinos, *French Odyssey. Greece in French Travel Literature from the Renaissance to the Romantic Era* (Baltimore and London: Johns Hopkins University Press, 1994), p. 198. Similar sentiments are expressed by such poets as Pushkin and Lamartine.

słońca nad Salaminą" ["Sunrise over Salamis"], the unpub-
lished Canto 9 of *Voyage*), it was more than natural to ask at
that point whether there was a real chance to rise again. If there
is a message in Słowacki's lines, it is the poet's call to keep the
warrior spirit alive. This reading seems consistent with the next
five stanzas (15–19), where the poet plunges into vehement
attacks against the Polish national character and the causes of
his country's death, finding guilt in everyone and assuming the
role of supreme judge of his nation.

Before we move to further analysis, let us point out an odd
fact: although Słowacki is looking for a Greek counterpart for
the place where Poland died (that is, Maciejowice), the grave
of the Greek state, Chaeronea, appears in *Agamemnon's Tomb*
only once. It is Thermopylae that constitutes the central place
of the poem and each time the poet invokes it, he gives us a
reason why his horse should not stop there. In other words, on
the one hand the resting place for his horse is to be a counter-
part where Greece died, and Thermopylae clearly is not that
place; on the other hand, the reasons why his horse cannot stop
at Thermopylae is that there Słowacki would have to account
for his nation's failure. This strange lack of parallelism begs
the following thought: Poland lost her independence, like
Greece, because of a lack of unity. However, Poland had a
chance to regain independence in 1830 (at least such was
Mochnacki's message) but failed because of lack of military
and political strategy and organization. Unlike the Poles, the
Ancient Greeks combined two things: the military valor at
Thermopylae with strategic genius at Salamis a year later.
Poles had the former but lacked the latter. And the reason for
this, as the poet explains at the end of the poem, with his image
of a blood-splattered moon, is the immature Romantic imagi-
nation which lies at the root of the failed uprising.

Part 4.

The "Jovial Skull" and the Naked Hero.

[15]
At Thermopylae a body lies
Without red cloak or golden sash.
It is the naked corpse of Leonidas:
A beautiful soul dwells in its marble form.
For a long time the people mourned his sacrifice,
The scented flame and the broken goblet.

[16]
O Poland! So long as your angelic soul
Is cased within a jovial skull,
So long will the executioner chop at your body,
Nor will your vengeful sword cause terror,
So long will you have a hyena prowling over you
And a grave to seize you – open-eyed!

These two stanzas should be read together in terms of contrast. Stanza 15 sets up a fairly conventional image of the heroic Leonidas: his marble corpse contains a "beautiful soul." The words "naked" and the whiteness suggested by "marble" indicate purity and classical perfection of form. The legacy of the Spartan king is likewise unambiguous; his people wept for a long time, appreciating his sacrifice. The absent garments Słowacki mentions – red cloak and golden sash – refer to specifically Polish clothing (see below). However, several visual elements invoked in these stanzas recall the famous painting of Leonidas by Jean-Louis David (completed 1814). A paragon of neo-classicism in art, the painting portrays the Greek hero calmly facing forward, unmoved by the fear we might expect. His body is nearly naked (an image of the "naked corpse" in Słowacki), adorned only by a bright red cloak and a golden sash – the two colors mentioned in the Leonidas passage of *Agamemnon's Tomb*.[1] It is as though Słowacki is emphasizing: this is not the canonical Leonidas of David and others.

The fire and broken goblet in stanza 15 are seemingly signs of ritual, possibly burial rites. The sounds in "czara" (goblet) anticipate those in "czerep" (skull/head), which has a second meaning of "bowl" or "goblet." The implication is that the fire allowed the goblet to break, which released the "beautiful soul" of Leonidas. Poland likewise needs to shatter its casing and be freed either by proper burial or apotheosis by fire. The themes of burial and fire leading to apotheosis recur in the next stanzas.

In this passage Słowacki famously condemns that national characteristic of Poles, the "jovial" (or "boorish") skull (*czerep rubaszny*). There is no way of rendering the term "czerep rubaszny" in English in an unambiguous way, but the phrase in Polish is ambiguous as well. The word "czerep" can mean

---

1   David's painting had strong associations with Napoleon when it was first exhibited, but was revisited in 1823 and later in connection with Botzaris and the Greek revolution. See Nina Athanassoglou-Kallmyer, *French Images from the Greek War of Independence, 1821–1830. Art and Politics under the Restoration* (New Haven and London: Yale University Press, 1989), p. 55.

head, skull, or shell. Słowacki's use of an antiquated word, instead of "głowa" (head) or "czaszka" (skull), gives it a special emphasis. However, the crucial point here is the adjective "rubaszny," which can be approximated in English by "jovial," "coarse," "boorish," "boisterous"; it also suggests lightheartedness or recklessness.

The other lines that demand explication are the first two: the golden belt ("złoty pas") and red cloak ("czerwony kontusz") are marks of the traditional costume of the Polish gentry, a direct reference to Polish "Sarmatism." The Polish nobility distinguished itself with the "kontusz," a robe-like garment, often tied with a gold or yellow sash. It was of Eastern origin, initially imported from Persia and Turkey. In addition, the Polish gentry wore their hair in a particular way: half-shaved, with moustache, and dressed in a luxurious robe. The combination of this hair style, the red cloak and the golden belt all create a visual image of the *rubaszny* (jovial) nobleman.[2]

The pure and naked figure of Leonidas, who represents heroism and self-sacrifice, introduces a striking contrast with the overdressed Sarmatian nobleman. The Sarmatian exterior

2   The significance as a visual marker of this vibrant clothing is addressed by Andrzej Waśko in his book *Romantyczny Sarmatyzm. Tradycja szlachecka w literaturze polskiej lat 1831–1863* [Romantic Sarmatism. The Tradition of the Nobility in Polish Literature in the Years 1831–1863] (Krakòw: Arcana, 1995) and "Romantic Sarmatism," in *Sarmatian Review*, XVII, 2. According to Waśko, for the generation just following the partitions of Poland, a nostalgic return to the traditions of the past had extra weight compared to the colorful "Medieval" nostalgia of Romanticism elsewhere (for example, in England or France). Seemingly at odds with the development of Western political ideas, in fact Sarmatism became a positive motif in Polish Romantic poetry. Whereas in the Enlightenment period in the eighteenth century the traditional gentry and their "red cloak" (*kontusz*) and "golden sash" were the objects of ridicule, they were treated with seriousness and warmth in such works as Mickiewicz's *Pan Tadeusz* and later in the epic historical novels of Henryk Sienkiewicz.

covers the beautiful and the true. The specificity of the allusion to clothing of the Polish nobility gives a clear reading: The "angelic soul" of (true) Poland is trapped inside a "sarmatian skull." The proper rendering of Słowacki's lines could be: "as long as your angelic soul remains imprisoned in this Sarmatian mentality."[3] The skull must be shattered to release the soul and enable Poland to be "whole" (to fight the executioner who is continuously dismembering the body); to take revenge (the sword must become "dreadful"); to fend off the foreign attackers (symbolized by the hyena prowling around the tomb); and, finally, to have a proper burial (eyes will be closed in the coffins; Polydorus in Virgil did not receive proper burial). The image of the corpse in perpetual desecration prepares, as we shall see, for the introduction of the persona of Prometheus in stanza 20.

In attacking the "czerep rubaszny" and "red kontusz" Słowacki launches an attack against the Sarmatian mentality of which the clothing is only an external expression. The true origin of this coarse mentality is political: the "golden liberty" of Polish nobility, with their right to elect their kings, and its corollary – the infamous *liberum veto*. Both of them constitute the essence of the nobleman's life, and both lie at the root of the historical process that gradually led to the partitions of Poland. In 1764, only twelve years before the first partition, in a letter to Anna Jabłonowska, Prince Karol Radziwiłł wrote: "I praise the Lord, believe not in the Devil, respect the law, *know*

---

3   Similar imagery is found elsewhere in Słowacki's work. For example, in *Poema Piasta Dantyszka*, Słowacki invokes again an image of a "Polish face" that is genuine and without a shell: "Po całym piekle niech słyszą szlachcica, Twarz polska nie ma obłudnej skorupy, Niechaj w nią patrzą jak w zwierciadło trupy" ("Let this nobleman's voice be heard all over Hell, the Polish face does not have an ugly shell, Let the dead look at it as if it was a mirror," ll. 530–532).

no king, because I am a nobleman with a free voice."[4] In no other country did the nobility feel equal to kings, and in no other country was the king's power so limited and paralyzed. The unbridled power of the Sarmatian gentry was directly proportional to the king's powerlessness.[5] Commentators recognize the critique of "czerep rubaszny" and "kontusz" as a call for reform. But in the face of the nonexistence of Poland as a country, what, besides a mentality, singled out here as "czerep rubaszny," could be a possible target of Słowacki's criticism? According to Tadeusz Sinko, it is the call to a "beautiful (à l'antique) deed, to a democratizing shedding of one's clothes, shaking off the chains."[6] Leszek Libera, opposing the previous "democratic" readings,[7] believes that: "In 1839 [. . .] Słowacki was not a utopian democrat. [. . .] There is no word 'peasant' or 'people' in the poem: there are only 'Poland' and 'nation.'"[8] Józef Tretiak makes yet another interesting remark: "If [Słowacki] hides anything behind this

---

4   Quoted in Zamoyski, *The Polish Way*, p. 201 (emphasis ours). As Zamoyski writes: "[T]he closest parallel to a Polish magnate's way of life at this time is to be found in that of an Indian maharaja" (Zamoyski, *ibid.*, p. 200).

5   *Ibid.*, p. 204.

6   Sinko, *Hellenizm Juliusza Słowackiego*, p. 114.

7   Libera, *Juliusza Słowackiego Podróż*, p. 117. Libera does not list Tadeusz Sinko, who shared the same interpretation, possibly because the latter was not, strictly speaking, a Polish literary scholar.

8   Libera, *Ibid.*, p.117. Libera adduces several other facts to support his claim. During his stay in Warsaw Słowacki was Prince Czartoryski's protégé, and during the 1830–1831 Uprising he was an employee of the Ministry of Foreign Affairs. Słowacki left Poland on March 8, 1831, in a hurry: "it appears that he had left as Czartoryski's subordinate . . . carrying Czartoryski's diplomatic post" (p. 86). What is more, in two of his works, the play *Kordian* and the narrative poem *Lambro*, Słowacki makes critical remarks about Joachim Lelewel and the party of the democrats. In addition, the poet's later voyage to the East very likely had a diplomatic character (p. 94).

symbol [the kontusz] it is probably the caste system of old Poland. But it was not the caste system, which was omnipresent in Europe, that led Poland to ruin, but the cult of disorderliness which made it more fatal [in Poland] than elsewhere."[9] If the focus of Słowacki's criticism is indeed Poland's social stratification, two questions arise: how much democratization, so to speak, does Słowacki demand? And, what kind of reforms does Słowacki have in mind given the fact that Poland had ceased to exist as a political entity? The latter question suggests that the object of Słowacki's criticism is not so much political institutions as the national character itself. The next stanzas appear to confirm this claim.

[17]
Cast off the last shred of those hideous rags,
That burning shirt of Deianira:
And rise, unashamed, like great statues,
Naked – washed in the mire of the Styx,
New – insolent in iron nakedness –
Not shamed by anything – immortal!

Whereas in the previous stanza Słowacki merely describes the fatal consequences of "kontusz" and "czerep," here the two merge into one: Deianira's (burning) shirt, which the poet calls Poland to tear off. Deianira refers to the wife of Heracles. Deianira's shirt is an allusion to the venom-saturated shirt, a gift from the centaur Nassus slaughtered by Heracles, that she gave her husband. Before he died, Nassus saturated the shirt in his blood telling Deianira that it would make Heracles faithful. The centaur's gift was a trick; his blood was venom that burnt

---

9   Józef Tretiak, *Juliusz Słowacki*, 2 vols. (Kraków: Akademia Umiejętności, 1904), vol. 1, p. 113.

the hero's body. Unable to find a cure, Heracles builds his funeral pyre and dies on it. In the *The Women of Trachis*, where we find the Heracles story, Sophocles evokes the pass of Thermopylae. The pass was named for its "burning waters," and according to myth the waters became burning after Heracles plunged into them in a vain effort to alleviate his agony. The Chorus in *The Women of Trachis* locates Heracles at Thermopylae ("hot passage") and alludes to the Spartan defeat, but does not speak of Heracles' torment as its source: "Safe harbor, hot-springs among the rocks [. . .] and there at the Gates, the famous gatherings of the Greeks" (ll. 633–639).[10] Herodotus describes the pass in terms of Heracles: "There are hot springs in the pass [. . .] with an altar over them dedicated to Heracles."[11] Heracles and his torment from the shirt are thus commonly linked with Thermopylae, the site Słowacki singles out in *Agamemnon's Tomb*.

The invocation of Deianira and implicitly Heracles can mean Heracles' suffering and death, but also his apotheosis and immortality Let us note that Słowacki evokes the image of the river Styx which, in Greek mythology, had two meanings: it made mortals immortal, and it was the force that punished the gods themselves when they made a false oath. Ovid alludes to the first, more familiar, meaning in Book XIV of *Metamorphoses*, where Venus convinces Jupiter and the other gods to make Aeneas immortal after his long life full of travails: the Styx waters "cleansed and washed quite away whatever was mortal in Aeneas" (XIV: ll. 581–607; 603–605).

10 Michael Jameson, trans., in David Grene and Richard Lattimore, eds., *Sophocles II. Ajax. The Women of Trachis. Electra. Philoctetes* (Chicago: University of Chicago Press, 1967). This allusion occurs before Heracles has put the shirt on, and thus before his suffering.

11 Herodotus, *Histories*, Book VII, p. 477. Herodotus also repeats the legend that Leonidas was a descendant of Heracles (p. 487), providing another link between the two legends.

Poland's invoked resurrection is thus a further connection to Aeneas and Troy, a traditional association in Polish thought since the Enlightenment.

Słowacki's overt attempt to impose Greek tragedy onto Polish history and a commentary on the contemporary situation allows us (even requires us) to seek a connection to his other interpretive angle on Polish history. Sophocles' tragedies may have provided him with a poetic model but he composed it based on his proto-Slavic mythological past.[12]

One could push the ambiguity of Słowacki's position even further. According to the logic of Słowacki's parallelism between the Weneds, the conquered people in *Lilla Weneda*, and the Ilots, Słowacki should address the Spartan helots, not the Spartan warriors, unless, of course, there is no such parallel and Słowacki has something else in mind. In *Agamemnon's Tomb*, Słowacki tells the Spartans that he comes from the country of the Ilots. However, the latter, as far as we know, have never had any virtues that the Spartans needed to survive or that would have contributed to the fabric of the Spartan way of life. Why is Słowacki invoking the word Ilot, suggesting "helot," when he addresses the Spartan warriors? If there is any logic to it, it must consist in that the masters (of Poland), the

12 Maria Kalinowska, "Słowackiego Greckie Sny o Polsce" ["Słowacki's Greek Dreams about Poland"]. According to Kalinowska, while *Agamemnon's Tomb* presents a synthesis of Polish and Greek history, "*Lilla Weneda*, was the last prophetic word of the chorus of the Polish history in the form of tragedy – not the Shakespearian tragedy, but the most ancient one – the Greek tragedy, Aeschylian one – the most primal and severe" (p.22). However, on a number of occasions Słowacki acknowledges his debt of gratitude to Euripides as his main inspiration. As he himself declares in Canto IV of the *Voyage*: "My beloved Euripides gave me the word of the Eumenides to declaim" (stanza [15], *Dzieła* [*Works*], vol. IV, 58). Similarly, he mentions Euripides as his inspiration in the preface to *Lilla Weneda* (*Dzieła* [*Works*], vol, VII, 288).

Lechs, ultimately failed and that the "Polish Sparta" became the "Ilotopolis" (foreign servant). To Kridl, in these two works "the shortcomings and vices of the contemporary generation became [. . .] explained and explicable. Hence one can easily understand the call for a "new Poland 'bathed in the Stygian mud,' because one cannot expect anything from a Poland burdened with the sins of the past."[13]

The immediate interpretation of stanza 17 is that Poland must cast off its false garments and be "true." However, if the garment was a trick played by the enemy in the ancient story (Nassus gave Deianira a deadly gift), and its donning thus an accident, Poles in this allusion imposed the deadly garment upon their body willingly. Słowacki is unambiguous on this point: "So long as your angelic soul/ Is cased within a jovial skull,/ So long will the executioner chop at your body." In other words, the work of dismembering Poland by foreign powers is a result of the Sarmatian mentality. Also, the elaborate system of imagery built around clothing and nakedness in the poem as a whole suggests that clothing is "false," "deadly," "crude," but first of all "someone else's feathers" (as the peacock and parrot, invoked in the next stanza, suggests).

[18]
Let the northern nation rise up from its silent grave
And frighten other people at the sight
Of such a huge statue – made from a single stone!
And so forged that it will never shatter in thunder,
But its hands and crown will be of lightning,
And a gaze scornful of death – the blush of life.

This stanza shows what Poland can become, once it casts off Deianira's shirt: glorious and powerful. The comparison of a

13 Manfred Kridl, *Antagonizm wieszczów*, pp. 178–179.

resurrected Poland to the statue leads us back to the statue of Leonidas invoked earlier. For this, however, this northern nation must be made of one piece.[14] Moreover, the image of forging suggests melting different elements into one. On the surface Słowacki's call to unity does not seem complicated. The unbridled individualism of the Polish nobility led to Poland's destruction; only re-forging it, making it one whole, can make it powerful again.

If one can translate Słowacki's poetic imagery into the language of social issues, we run again into the same question: what kind of unity does Słowacki have in mind? Does he mean unity of the nation, which would overcome its social stratification? If so, was Słowacki on the side of radical social reformers, such as Mochnacki, or the moderate democrats? Or, is his criticism confined to the émigré parties and politicians?[15] Slowacki read his poem at the Polish Literary Society only a week after Prince Adam Czartoryski delivered his annual address there on November 29, 1839. In his address Czartoryski had called for the national unity of the emigration: "But who does not know that lack of agreement and anarchy

14 By referring to Poland as the "northern nation" Słowacki is invoking a popular trope of early Romanticism. Mme de Staël's *On Germany* set the ground to divide Europe between north and south, with the northern nations (Germany, England, Scotland) identified as more primitive yet more "original," less burdened by the need to imitate France. A crucial Polish variant on this theme was written by Maurycy Mochnacki in 1825, "O duchu i źrodłach poezji" ["On the Spirit and Sources of Poetry"] (in *Idee Programowe Romantyków Polskich*, pp., 93–100). It is likely that Słowacki would know both works, but probably Mochnacki is the immediate source of this allusion to the "northern nation" in this stanza.

15 In Libera's view: "Emigration brought to the fore, like a prism, all the Sarmatian vices: the plague of drunkenness, duels, bickering, blustering, and unbridled individualism. There is no reason to look for plans of social reforms in the poem." *Juliusza Słowackiego Podróż*, pp. 118–119.

destroyed Poland, and they can even perpetuate this destruction more easily? All of us are convinced of this and all, regardless of their party, call for agreement and unity, a unity which can join together broken parts . . . [and bring] more power to the whole, which would increase the likelihood of the desired effect."[16] According to Libera, the Society was a camouflage "political party" led by Prince Adam Czartoryski himself.[17] Słowacki was introduced to the Society in May, 1839 by the Prince's close friend, Count Roman Załuski, so "It would have been a faux pas and a demonstration of ignorance to present in his declamation a social program of the opposing camp."[18]

Libera buttresses his view of Słowacki as opposing the program of democratic camp with considerable evidence. However, he seems to confuse cause and effect when he writes: "The general critique of the nobility's vices, Sarmatism, is not tantamount to the rejection of the traditional Polish political model."[19] But it was within this "traditional model" that the vices were allowed to flourish.[20] And if Słowacki was in the least sympathetic to it, what was his point in criticizing "czerep rubaszny"? The system of *liberum veto* and the electoral king

16 *Mowy Księcia Adama Czartoryskiego od roku* 1838–1847 [Speeches by Prince Adam Czartoryski, 1838–1847 (Paris, 1847), pp. 6–7. Quoted in Libera, *ibid.*, p.120.

17 *Ibid.*, p. 117.

18 *Ibid.* p. 117.

19 *Ibid.*, p. 118.

20 In his later period, Słowacki writes in a letter to George Sand (*Dzieła* [*Works*] XIV, p. 369): "We were heralds of the freedom of the individual conscience; our fathers felt sufficient power of creating according to Divine laws – a new human form. They failed and suffer not because they were too small or wretched but because they could not measure up to the demands of their own spirit. Not being able to achieve this unanimity [perfect consensus] through love, they craved to reach it in desperation through human means – they used that [liberum] veto the way angels used the heavenly fire, to their own perdition."

imposed few or no restraints on them. The vices, as Jòzef Tretiak observes, led to the unbridled license of the Polish gentry.[21] Just to quote an opinion of an English doctor who lived at the Polish court for ten years: "It is certain had we in England but the third part of their liberty, we could not live together without cutting one another's throats."[22] Słowacki may be restrained in his criticism of nobility for the reasons that Libera has advanced (the speech was given at the Prince Czartoryski's Literary Society). He may not have use the word "peasantry" and a few crucial terms that would make it unambiguous as to what exactly his social views are. And indeed it would have been a "faux pas" to overtly attack the class to which Czartoryski belonged. But one should also note that Czartoryski did not possess the vices of the class he belonged to, and he himself had criticized them only a week before Słowacki presented *Agamemnon's Tomb*.

Libera's contention is also dubious for another reason. In *Beniowski*, published a year later (in 1841), Słowacki launched his criticism with full force and in a way that outraged many of his readers, including Słowacki scholar Józef Tretiak. According to Tretiak, Słowacki is responsible for bringing back

---

21 In his revisionist work on Polish Romanticism, *Romantyczny Sarmatyzm* [Romantic Sarmatism], Andrzej Waśko, who is generally sympathetic to the Sarmatian theme in Romanticism, states: "The distance between the ironic and accusative tone of the judgments expressed in [*Lilla Weneda* and *Agamemnon's Tomb*] and the opinions from later years is the measure of distance Slowacki traveled from the anti-sarmatian position to the rehabilitation of the 'golden liberty' [of the gentry] in his work *Genezis z ducha*" (p. 26). In Waśko's view, "the Lechs are the encoded evaluation of the Polish gentry [. . .]. The romantics believed that the so-called fairytales in their mythical-symbolic form contain the key to the entire later history of the nation. Accordingly, the Lechs from *Lilla Weneda* are a brave and impulsive nation but not eager to reflect on the political consequences of their actions" (pp. 25–26).

22 *Ibid.* 204.

to life the shameful legend fabricated by the Prussians and Russians according to which Kościuszko in 1794, just before he was wounded, exclaimed: "Finis Poloniae" ("Poland is finished").[23] Recall, in *Agamemnon's Tomb* Słowacki is looking for a grave where his horse could rest. To achieve the absoluteness of the equation between Greece and Poland, Słowacki needs a battleground that would be the counterpart of Maciejowice. Just like Greece at Chaeronea in 338 B.C., Poland lost its political independence at Maciejowice in 1794. The last partition, in 1795, was the proverbial nail in the coffin.

The "poetry" of the words "Finis Poloniae" could give this equation between the two national graves a dramatic texture. Why did Słowacki not include "Finis Poloniae" in

---

23   The legend originated in 1794. In *Süd-preussische Zeitung* (Nr. 24), one could read that the last words of the wounded Kosciuszko were reported as: *Finis Poloniae* (*Poland is finished*). And indeed, the next year, Poland was erased from the map of Europe. How was it possible, Tretiak asks Słowacki, to know what Kościuszko had said if there was no one around him except the attacking Cossacks? Did Kościuszko make a theatrical gesture before being almost mortally wounded speaking in Latin to the enemies? As Kościuszko himself confessed to his friend Niemcewicz, upon being released from the Russian prison after twenty-six months, when he saw the approaching Cossacks, he put a pistol in his mouth wanting to kill himself. The pistol, however, did not fire! The *Finis Poloniae* legend was fabricated and considered by patriotic Poles to be a shameful anecdote fabricated by Poland's enemies. Its purpose was to break the spirit of national resistance and make the Poles accept the inevitable: Poland is finished! The reaction of *Finis Poloniae* was the song – which became the Polish national anthem – composed by Kościuszko's General, Józef Wybicki: "Jeszcze Polska nie zginęła, pòki *my* żyjemy . . ." The detail of the peregrinations of the *Finis Poloniae* can be found in a Józef Tretiak's fascinating account: *Finis Poloniae. Historia legendy maciejowickiej i jej rozwiązanie* [*Finis Polaniae. History of Maciejowice Legend and Its Development*] (Kraków: Krakowska Spółka Wydawnicza, 1921), esp. p. 67. See also Janion and Żmigrodzka's more recent discussion in their *Romantyzm i historia*, pp. 276–303.

Agamemnon's Tomb? There are several possibilities. First, on December 5, 1839, when Słowacki presented his poem for the first time at the Literary Society in Paris, he was stepping forth as a national bard. If Tretiak is correct that the anecdote was as unpalatable to the Polish émigrés in Paris as it is to him, Słowacki was probably careful not recall it publicly as the anecdote also had a considerable currency among people hostile to the Polish cause. However, a year later, irritated and angry at the lack of his success as the first bard,[24] Słowacki lost his temper and attacked everyone. He invoked Kościuszko and Maciejowice again, making the Polish-American hero say: "Kościuszko przeczuł was, krzycząc: *skończona!*" ("Kościuszko foresaw you when he exclaimed: [Poland is] finished.") To translate this loosely: "Kościuszko knew what you truly represent: Poland died because of you." If one places Słowacki's comments in the context of the Insurrection, and the social reforms – reform of serfdom, conscription of peasants –initiated by Kościuszko, his criticism of Deianira's shirt is more fitting when referring to the vices of nobility and the old Poland's political system than to a handful of émigrés.[25]

24 For the story of rivalry between Słowacki and Mickiewicz, see Wiktor Weintraub, "A Duel of Improvisations," in *Studies in Russian and Polish Literature in Honor of Wacław Lednicki*, edited by Z. Folejewski (The Hague: Mouton, 1962), pp. 142–159.

25 Słowacki might have felt more sympathy for Czartoryski's camp, rather than for Mochnacki's radical "republicanism" or Lelewel's "democracy." However, if Libera's claim that there is no evidence to place Slowacki on the side of the republicans or democrats is true, he is grossly overstating his case by presenting Slowacki as someone having a particular insight into politics. Słowacki's letters, particularly from the late period, suggest that the poet's understanding of politics was somewhat childish, to put it mildly, and his letters from the so-called mystical period indicate that the poet started losing his senses.
   In 1847, Slowacki considered Homer (!) to be the source of true political insight. He presented his ideas in a serious speech during the pro-

The above reading is, however, merely circumstantial and does not stem from the text of the poem itself. In our opinion the reason for not including the "Finis Poloniae" is purely structural. Słowacki develops this theme in Canto IV ("On Greece"). In this canto he mentions Kościuszko in stanza 22, and in 44 he directly equates the Greek Chaeronea and the Polish Maciejowice: "O Cheroneo . . . , O Maciejowice." Why did Słowacki not include it *Agamemnon's Tomb?* Most likely because its inclusion would have destroyed the pathos of Greece and its military genius; but also, it would minimize the blame for the November Uprising, which was not an "objective fact" but the result of a failed strategy.[26] In other words, recalling Chaeronea would have moved the reader away from Greek (Spartan) bravery at Thermopylae, symbolizing the unity of the Greeks and, indirectly, the victory at Salamis, to later Greek

ceedings of "The Historical and Literary Society" on November 4, 1847. The Secretary of the Society thought of it as humorous and a reflection of Słowacki's "ability to make comparisons, what the Germans call Witz." Słowacki did not mean it as "Witz" and repeated it, again, in the form of a call to form a confederation. See Sinko, *Hellenizm Juliusza Słowackiego*, p. 150.

See also Norman Davies' very well written summary of the influence of Romantic poetry and Mickiewicz and Słowacki's influence, in his *Heart of Europe*, pp. 220–221. Słowacki did not become a leader the way Mickiewicz did for his generation, but his poetry became inspiring for the generation to come. "In 1863–1864, the insurgents paid homage to Słowacki. 'In the climate of opinion preceding the January Rising,' Janion and Żmigrodzka write, 'Romanticism of the mystical vintage achieved its widest social response and played an especially important role . . . [Słowacki's] mystical works formed the setting for the conduct of the new generation in the course of its historical testing-time; his personality molded it; and his statements during the Springtime of Nations in 1848 were well known to all his admirers.'" Davies, *ibid.*, p. 234.

26 Among contemporary historians, Stanisław Łojek in his *Szanse powstania listopadowego* [The Chances of the November Uprising] maintains that the Uprising could have been won.

bickering and their final defeat. By the same token, recalling "Finis Poloniae" in *Agamemnon's Tomb* would have suggested that the two nations had similar histories and similar ends for similar reasons. In short, to talk about Chaeronea would mean to talk about "Finis Graeciae" and indirectly suggest that there was no chance for victory in the future either.

The historical analogies between Poland and Greece which the poet forces on the reader do not offer an easy reading as to what exactly is his point. The poet engages in a reflection over the fate of Greece and the conversation with the Spartans on the one hand and the failed 1830 November Uprising on the other. It is likely that Słowacki was trying to revive the military spirit in Poles by shaming them – this is sort of what Lord Byron did when he called on the modern Greeks to remember the glory of their ancient predecessors. Byron's influence – both poetic (his language and imagery), and biographical (his travel) – transpires in the poem and it is probable that "Byron's satellite" (as Sinko calls Słowacki, who was following in Byron's footsteps, both literally and poetically), recalled the British poet's words addressed to the Greeks and reshaped them for the Poles.

There was a difference, of course. The British poet addressed the Greeks before their own fight for national independence, and so the comparison of the modern Greeks to helots (Słowacki's Ilots) could indeed have had a revitalizing psychological effect: "Shades of the Helots! [. . .] Thy glorious day is o'er, but not they years of shame" (*Childe Harold's Pilgrimage*, LXXVI). It was a way of reminding them the days of ancient bravery and glory. However, if Słowacki indeed was thinking of and retrieving Byron –the Byron from over twenty years before Słowacki's own trip to Greece[27] – only to emulate

---

27   For background on the reception of Byron in the later romantic movements of Russia and Poland, see Catherine O'Neil, "Childe Harold in Crimea. The Byronic Sea Voyage in Russian and Polish Romanticism," in *Keats-Shelley Journal*, Vol. LVI, 2007, pp. 78–110.

his experience as a poet, he missed the point. For one, Byron was addressing a people before their fight and shaming them by offering them a vision meant to inspire them; doing the same to the Poles nine years after the national tragedy, could not have the same effect. It was tactless and at best it was a kind of a poetic faux pas on his part.[28]

We will see the poet making a similar faux pas in the next stanza.

28 Józef Tretiak, one of Słowacki's greatest scholars, was highly critical of the poet's insensitivity and lack of grace. Commenting on the genesis of *Agamemnon's Tomb*, Tretiak writes: "A ray of sunlight came into the tomb and reminded the poet of Homer's harp's string, which he celebrated at the very outset of the poem:

"O! How far off sounds that golden harp,
Whose eternal echo is all that I hear!"

And it reminded him at the same time that he has a golden harp, that he is a Homer, but where's his fame? Where are his listeners? The deeper his momentary humiliation before the nothingness of centuries the more potent his desire for fame boiled in his chest. This desire shakes him from his meditations and makes him jump on the horse, makes him run to Thermopylae and Chaeronea, in order to throw the thunder of castigation at his nation, and at the same time reveal himself to his nation as its bard, summoning it to a new path [. . .] In considering the reasons for the poor reception of his poetry Słowacki came to the conclusion that it lies in the low intellectual development of his nation. He – Byron, Ariosto, the Polish Shakespeare – shining with a thousand shades, was unable to move Polish hearts [. . .] It could be the poet's own fault: namely, his lack of social sensitivity (a quality Mickiewicz possessed to the highest degree, and which Słowacki did not grasp) [. . .] The poet, full of adoration for himself, and inclined to his own self-elevation, did not hesitate to believe it. Having condemned his society in relationship to himself, he found the desire to condemn Poland both patriotically and politically." Tretiak, *Juliusz Słowacki*, 2 vols. (Kraków: Akademia Umiejętności, 1904), vol. 1, p. 108–109.

Part 5.

Poland – the Parrot and Peacock of Nations

[19]
O Poland, you are stilled fooled by trinkets;
You have been the peacock and parrot of nations,
And now you are a foreign servant.
Although I know these words won't resonate long
In your heart – where thought does not stay for even an
hour.
I say this because I am sad – and I myself am full of guilt.

This stanza is a strange mixture of elements: Poland is
someone else's servant or maid (służebnica) because Poland
was an imitator (parrot) and, perhaps, a vain fop (a
peacock).[1] The peacock, with his fancy and colorful tail, sug-
gests rich ostentatious dress, such as the "kontusz" (cloak)

---

1   Symbolically, besides referencing imitation, the parrot is a symbol of
    lasciviousness. It is enough to recall Tiepolo's painting, "The Death of
    Hyacinth," where the parrot looks over the dead body of Hyacinth, who
    was killed by Zephyrus because of lust; Hyacinth chose to love Apollo,
    and Zephyrus in his jealousy killed him.

and sash. Again, the image brings to mind the sarmatian nobleman.

Scholarship on this stanza has focused mainly on the 18th-and 19th-century debates concerning "pernicious" foreign influences in Poland. Słowacki's later obsessive hatred of France and everything French has additionally encouraged scholars to read these lines as the same criticism of foreign, particularly Western, influences, that he expresses in the 1840s. Libera goes so far as to suggest that Słowacki has in mind 19th-century ideologies: utopian socialism, democracy, Saint-Simonism, and the doctrines of Fourier and Owen. If the inclusion of contemporary political trends may be justified, it is only because of the poet's use of the present tense in the first line: "trinkets still deceive you." However, one could argue that the use of the present tense is not a reference to anything specific (and the poem itself does not suggest this either, for that matter), but is an expression of the poet's general assessment of the Polish mind which is susceptible to imitation.

Criticism of imitation in the name of "what is genuinely Polish" was widespread in the 18th century, and it often took the form of the contention that Poland perished because it "adopted too many foreign influences." Such criticism, however, is devoid of serious argumentative substance. Here is a sample of such reasoning: "Why should the Poles look for social education among foreigners. . . . Poland died because it became all too foreign [scudzoziemczała] [. . .] Poland will not rise again except by shedding its foreign elements, that is, by returning to its faith and virtues, its nationality."[2] The prototype of this kind

2 A. Jełowiecki, "O duchu narodowym" ("On National Spirit"), *Dzieła* [*Works*], vol. VI, pp. 64–65. (Quoted in Libera, *Juliusza Słowackiego Podróż*, p. 121.) On the theme of imitation and the specificity of Polishness, see Jerzy Jedlicki, *A Suburb of Europe: Nineteenth-Century Polish Approaches to Western Civilization* (Budapest: Central European University Press, 1999), pp. 3–45.

of reasoning is Cato the Elder, who is described by Plutarch as defending Roman virtues against Greek education. Similar statements to this can be found in the writings of virtually every nation, particularly a nation assailed by a psychological crisis of identity or when the national identity is under attack. The problem becomes particularly pertinent in the political context of the second half of the 18th century. There is little disagreement between historians that the "genuinely" Polish political system of *liberum veto* and electoral kings were the two major factors that made partition of Poland possible. The political organization of Poland in the 17th and 18th centuries was reminiscent of the papal conclave, which requires unanimity,[3] whereas the world outside this "medieval" realm was moving in the direction of a majority principle and parliamentary government with limited royal powers. If we look at the means employed to save Poland from collapse, such as the Constitution of May 3rd[4], the famous Committee of National Education, the introduction of classical learning of which Prince Czartoryski was a champion and the curator for the Vilnius region, none can be said to deserve criticism, let alone can they be considered as perniciouson the grounds they were an imitation of something "foreign."

The clash between the Enlightenment reformers and the "traditionalists" manifested itself strongly on a psychological

---

3   Andrzej Walicki in *The Slavophile Controversy* writes: "In fact the unanimity which was binding on the Russian village self-government was only one of the survival of the medieval *unanimitats*, an archaic form of corporate will which was gradually, though not without a lengthy struggle, superseded in Europe by the principle of majority decisions" (p. 262).

4   A very enlightening discussion of the Polish Constitution in the context of the "sarmatian culture" of Poland of that period can be found in Rett R. Ludwikowski's "The Firsts: A Comparative Study of the American and the Polish Constitutions," in: *Michigan Yearbook of International Legal Studies*, Vol. VII, 1987, pp. 117–156.

level. In an article called "The Constitution of 3rd May," written in *Pielgrzym* (*Pilgrim*), we read:

> In the end, this [foreign-A.Waśko] spirit had subjected to mockery national customs and national dress, and by attacking the ancestral faith discouraged a great number of noble members of the parliament, who saw on the one side the muscovite party, and on the other patriots dressed in frockcoats and wigs, with [busts of] Rousseau and Montesquieu in their hands, holding up to ridicule their shaved heads, their customs, their way of speaking. They became discouraged and did not do much, and in this way they did great damage to their country.[5]

Słowacki's position is even more difficult to understand if one realizes that Słowacki is criticizing both "czerep rubaszny" (Poland's traditional vices) and imitation, which, according to the reformers, was supposed to counteract those vices. In launching an attack against imitation Słowacki would be attacking the reformers, which would put him in a position critical of the Czartoryski family, traditionally referred to as the "Familia," the leaders of the 18th century reforms. On the other hand, his criticism of "czerep rubaszny" places him on the side of the Czartoryskis and their contempt for the masses of minor nobility and their sarmatian customs. In other words, criticism of the two opposing attitudes expressed by these key terms – imitation and "czerep rubaszny" – in this stanza looks like an inconsistency on Słowacki's part.

This inconsistency can be minimized, however, by taking Słowacki's position not to be a reference to a party program but, rather, as a general critical assessment of national character which oscillated between the two. While the former may be said to extol one's own as possessing intrinsic value because it is

---

5   Quoted in A. Waśko, *Romantyczny sarmatyzm*, p. 55.

one's own, the latter points to the inability of forming a judgment, and attaching a higher value on everything that comes from abroad. The act of imitation is an intellectual trait that attaches value not only to "foreign" objects as better or more valuable than one's own, but on a deeper level it is an admission of having little creative powers, or the inability to find enough creative energy in oneself and one's own tradition.

In a letter to his father sent from Florence, January 26, 1836, Zygmunt Krasiński, the third "national bard" of Poland and Słowacki's close friend, made a remark that sheds light on Słowacki's criticism in *Agamemnon's Tomb*.

We have been the most insecure, the most errant and the most pallid nation in the history of man, so to speak [. . .] nations and crowns could have been ours, and we did not know how to take advantage of anything. We could not seize any opportunity when it presented itself. When was a Pole an ingenious politician? [. . .] Have we achieved anything in the sciences, in crafts and arts? [. . .] Is there Polish poetry, architecture or painting or music? Have we contributed anything Polish to the world other than vulgar joviality [*rubaszność*]? – Our clothing came first from Western Europe; later it was borrowed from the Orient [. . .] the Polish nation has always been slow to launch war, or summon troops called on by the king; it liked comfort too much. However, it is a great swaggerer [cf "peacock"]; and only someone who falls short of having something boasts of what he does not have – he is like an ape, because he imitates what is not his [. . .] we wasted everything, not because of generosity, not because of incontinence, not because of unbridled passions, but because of a lack of reason, and sometimes lack of heart . . . it was this principle that took root in Poland and destroyed all ground for poetry; the buffoonish principle, the gentry's *rubaszność*, courtly uncleanness, love of power. –In other nations there were special men who were to satisfy this buffoonish principle; they were called royal jesters. [. . .] With us the entire gentry practiced this craft.[6]

In an earlier letter to his father, written on March 21, 1830, Krasiński wrote:

> An unfortunate will to slavishly ape others has destroyed us, Poles, in today's literary epoch; if not all of us, at least quite a few, and particularly those who imitated Byron[7] or another poet... Schlegel beautifully says [in *Geschichte der alten und neuen Literatur*], that like our religion, so our poetry – clearly, Romanticism is our newer and genuine poetry – it springs from between graves and hence its tendency to melancholy, to feelings about another world and more sublime thought than classical ideas, because the classicists understood merely carnal beauty and we understood spiritual beauty.

The kernel of Krasiński's criticism is the same as what we find in Słowacki. However, it expands on what Słowacki's succinct poetic language cannot. "Rubaszność" is linked to creative paralysis and vulnerability. As such, a "rubaszny" nation is doomed to imitate.

Nowhere did Słowacki express his concerns with imitation in the sense of vulnerability with more force than in his review of Bohdan Zaleski's poetry, published in *Młoda Polska* ("Young Poland"), a journal sympathetic to Mickiewicz and highly critical of Słowacki's poetry. Słowacki begins his review with a description of Raphael's painting of the Madonna, which became a subject of many imitations in Germany. What in childlike simplicity was a stroke of a genius

---

6 Quoted in Józef Tretiak, *Juliusz Słowacki*. Vol. 1, pp. 110–111.
7 A similar sentiment was expressed by Słowacki in his *Beniowski*, Canto I [25] (*Poland's Angry Romantic*, p. 177). See footnote 109 below.

in Raphael became, according to Słowacki, kitsch. It makes one think that in creating it "one achieved the peak of artistry." "This comparison fully applies to the Catholic simplicity of Mr. Zeleski's [poem] 'Przegrawki.'" There is no point in discussing further Słowacki's merciless review of the poem which, he goes on to say, can be understood by simple minds who do not understand the meaning of great poetry. In *Beniowski*, published roughly a year after *Agamemnon's Tomb*, Słowacki returns to his criticism of *Młoda Polska* writers, concluding ironically that since "my nation is afraid of blank verse, I must rhyme with Tasso's rhyme."

At one point, however, Słowacki takes on the great Polish Renaissance poet, Jan Kochanowski, whom he will praise in stanza 30 in *Agamemnon's Tomb*: "A nice nobleman; our language owes him a lot, but our thought owes him nothing." Słowacki's criticism of Kochanowski comes as a surprise given the stature of Kochanowski as the father figure of the Polish Renaissance. But Słowacki's point is clear: poetry creates a soul of a nation; it provides sustenance for it, and *now*, after Poland ceased to exist as a country, poetry is a vehicle of national survival;[8] the simplicity of poetic words, no matter how beautiful, "is merely a sound."[9]

---

8   In his second letter to Prince Czartoryski, Słowacki writes: "even after the bodily resurrection, your Highness, there would be no true Poland" (*Dzieła* [*Works*], vol. XII p. 137). It is clear from Słowacki's many remarks that the spirit is all there is; people without souls would not be nations.

9   Słowacki, *Dzieła*, vol. XI, p. 145. One needs to note here Słowacki's agreement with Mochnacki. In "O Literaturze polskiej w wieku XIX" ["On Polish Literature in the 19th Century"] (*Idee programowe polskich romantykow*, pp. 137–138), Mochnacki states: "In a certain respect literature is the conscience of a nation. Hence, a nation that does not have an original literature, which has not brought forth its images, ideas and thoughts, is merely a collection of individuals, circumscribed by [geographical] borders, without being a moral collective."

In this review Słowacki mentions Kochanowski and Mickiewicz in the same breath, praising them for the beauty of their language.[10] "Mickiewicz's genius lies in his Midas-like power with words – sometimes a painter, who changes into a poet; when it comes to words, he is a Midas of color . . . Dante, Victor Hugo . . . a musician who turns into a poet, who finds unimaginable forms of sounds."[11] However, in the same letter he strikes at the very heart of Mickiewicz's poetry: "The whole of [Mickiewicz's] *Pan Tadeusz* comes down to idolatry of the piggishness of country life."[12] In other words, "rubaszność," the main object of attack in *Agamemnon's Tomb*, is the essence of Mickiewicz's greatest poem.[13]

10 Słowacki, *Dzieła* [*Works*, vol. XI, p. 144.
11 "Raptularz," *Dzieła* [*Works*], vol. XI, 210.
12 "Raptularz," *Dzieła* [*Works*], vol. XI, p. 226.
13 It may sound like a paradox but it would appear that if Mickiewicz, not Słowacki, became the national bard, it was because he was capable of expressing in his poetry, particularly in *Pan Tadeusz*, a longing for the lost (sarmatian) world and of giving the nation without a country what was needed most to survive: a link to its past. If we accept the thesis that literature perpetuates national vices and virtues, Mickiewicz can be said to be culpable for doing exactly that. His book-length poem became Poland's "national Bible" until the present day. However, we may also ask whether Poles would have survived for 126 years without a country had they not had Mickiewicz's "Bible."

Part 6.
"I say this because
I am full of guilt myself."

The line that ends the stanza about the parrot and peacock – "I say this because I am full of guilt myself" – is the most notoriously misread line in the whole poem. Most commentators read this statement as the poet's confession of guilt for not participating in the November Uprising. Libera modifies this reading by claiming that Słowacki is blaming himself for having chosen the wrong political alliances. Both views seem untenable.

In his *History of Polish Literature*, Czesław Miłosz points to this stanza in Słowacki, seeing in it a reflection of Słowacki's personality: "Some lines that have become proverbial show Słowacki's typical aggressiveness in his attitude toward his country. He conceived it his patriotic duty to castigate Poland for being 'the peacock and parrot' of other nations, and he searches for her 'angelic soul' imprisoned as it were in the skull of a drunken guffawing nobleman."[1] But was it

1   Czesław Miłosz, *The History of Polish Literature* (Berkeley: University of California Press, 1983), p. 238.

Słowacki's personal aggressiveness that prompted him to castigate his nation? Almost a century ago, Stanisław Stroński observed in a brief note that in throwing his invectives against Poland, Słowacki was merely imitating Dante, who in "Purgatory," Canto VI, exclaims: "O slavish Italy, the home of grief,/ship without pilot caught in a raging storm,/No queen of provinces – whorehouse of shame!" (ll. 76–78).[2] Stroński does not go much beyond noting this similarity before dropping the issue of Dante's influence on Słowacki altogether. However, it is worth examining the rhetorical similarity in greater depth. For example, in another stanza in the same Canto Dante says: "O wretched Italy, search all your coasts,/Probe to your very center; can you find/Within you any part that is at peace?" (ll. 85–87). And: "For all the towns of Italy are filled/with tyrants; any dolt who plays the role/of partisan can pass for a Marcellus" (ll. 124–126). Finally, Italy is compared to a sick old woman who, to escape pain and discomfort, cannot "stay quietly on her bed" (ll. 149–150). This image of a woman restlessly changing positions is a reference to the Italians' habit of constantly changing laws: "by the time November is half done/the laws spun in October are in shreds" (ll.143–144). In other words, Italians did not grasp what the ancient Greeks did: "Athens and Lacedemon, still well known/For ancient laws and civil discipline,/Showed but the finest signs of order then/Compared to you" (ll.139–142).

According to Dante, lack of "civil discipline" – that is, respect for laws as something above the individual will – had turned some Italian city-states into tyrannies. (The city-state structure common to Italy and Greece must have made the

2   Stanisław Stroński, "Wpływ Dantego w 'Grobie Agamemnona'" [Dante's Influence in "Agamemnon's Tomb"], *Pamiętnik Literacki*, vol. 8, 1909, pp. 152–157.

analogy between those countries easier for Dante.) Laws are enacted in the name of political stability, not comfort – something the "old woman," Italia, to ease her pain, disregards despite her illness. If Słowacki transposed Dante's insight in Canto VI to *Agamemnon's Tomb*, Słowacki may have understood the reason for the Poles' loss of statehood as being similar to the causes of tyranny in the Italian city-states. It was the golden liberty, that is, the gentry's refusal to accept any higher authority than its own will, or, making their will the law, that created conditions for the excessive individualism and license that cost Poland her statehood.[3]

Another similarity with Dante is a parallel between the transition from October to November in Dante and Słowacki's contrast between "heart" and "brains" in the following stanza of *Agamemnon's Tomb*. The heart, the seat of passion, is constantly changing and cannot contain a thought that lasts. As seasons change in Dante, passions change in Słowacki. The contents of the stanza do not allow for reading Słowacki as repeating Dante's criticism of changing laws; but his preceding remarks about the parrot and peacock suggest that the object of Słowacki's criticism is infirmity of judgment. Imitation means following a fashion; what is fashionable today is out of fashion tomorrow.

There is no logical reason to see in the last line of this stanza – "I say this because I am full of guilt." – a confession of guilt for not participating in the November Uprising. The context does not suggest any connection with this theme. The stanza is about the "national vice" of imitation and Słowacki's "confession" of guilt must be read against those words. Słowacki's fascination with Byron and Romanticism is well known; so is his criticism and rejection of Byron and

---

3   One should note here that in a later period Słowacki rejected the critical position he held in 1839. Walicki claims (although he does not give his source) that Słowacki saw the *liberum veto* as a bulwark of individualism against the majority rule. See *The Slavophile Controversy*, p. 263.

Romanticism's moral relativism.[4] Similarly, Słowacki's criticism of Mickiewicz's *Konrad Wallenrod* is clearly stated in *Beniowski*, where we find a dubious moral code that does not allow readers to distinguish between a patriot and traitor.[5] Therefore, Słowacki seems to be saying that in imitating

4   In *Beniowski*, Canto I [25] (*Poland's Angry Romantic*, p. 177), Słowacki writes:

O melancholy! Nymph! Whence comest though?
Art though a creeping plague, an epidemic?
From where didst though originate, and how?
Both noblemen and poets academic
Are touched by thee! – Ah, Nymph! I must avow
That I too caught the malady systemic,
And am by now (the devil! – I'm no ironist)
No longer Polish – but a Byronist . . .

In his "Słowacki – przeciwnik romantykòw" [Słowacki – a foe of Romantics], p. 71, Jarosław Maciejewski states: "The tragic youth who followed Romanticism, who – indecisive and immature, confused and alienated – led the whole nation to catastrophe, could be judged, naturally, in this very manner only after 1831. [. . .] He considered himself back then and later to be a man susceptible to this all-powerful erroneous and harmful poetic fashion."

5   The problematic hero of *Wallenrod* is inspired by a Lithuanian bard to recall his origins and betray the Teutonic Knights, the order which had fostered his career but which he now considers his enemy. He ends up destroying his former benefactors in the name of nationalism. Cf. M. Aronson, "'Konrad Vallenrod' i 'Poltava'," *Vremennik Pushkinskoi komissii*, vyp. 2 (1936), 43–56. Słowacki was suspicious of the "methodology" of betrayal. In *Beniowski*, Canto II [29] (*Poland's Angry Romantic*, p. 210) he writes:

Being like Wallenrod ("Wallenrodism")
Produced a mighty heap of good, I would claim!
It introduced a useful methodism –
From one a hundred thousand traitors came;
(Here I don't have a rhyme for my "-odism",
And as for "Ordiarlo", it's a shame,
It will be replaced by the Polish word:
"Wallenrodism" will soon be preferred).

Byron, Mickiewicz and Romanticism in his earlier works, he himself is "guilty" of the national vice he condemns the Polish nation for. However, there is also a structural reason – even a necessity – for Słowacki to place the words expressing guilt in the sentence ending this stanza. The next stanza introduces the Eumenides, the ancient Greek Furies whose function was to punish mortals for the most horrible of all crimes: matricide and parricide. *Agamemnon's Tomb* is about the death of the fatherland and, on a symbolic level, about those who committed this crime. In the next few stanzas Słowacki assumes several roles: he is Orestes the avenger as well as Orestes the victim; he is also the Eumenides. The admission of guilt is therefore required by the logic of the poem. The line about entering the "druidic" Agamemnon's tomb at the very beginning of the poem implies that the poet is not entering the Greek realm, but the Polish tomb, the realm of Polish history built around the ancient Greek story of the cycle of crimes that Słowacki found in the Oresteia trilogy.

If Słowacki's comparison of Poland to a parrot and peacock sounded offensive to Polish ears, as Miłosz states, one can only wonder how much more offensive Dante's comparison of Italy to a "whorehouse of shame" must have sounded to his fellow Italians.

Part 7.
A Polish Oresteia.
Literary Messianism.

[20]
Curse me – for my soul, like the Eumenides,
Runs you through the snaky gauntlet,
For you are Prometheus' only son:
The vulture doesn't eat your heart; it eats your brains.
Although I stain my muse with your blood,
I'll reach to your guts – and pull with all my might.

The Orestes theme in this climactic stanza combines with Prometheus to form a double image of the poet as agent of vengeance or justice.

The Eumenides (Słowacki) force their victim (Poland) to run "the gauntlet of snakes": "my soul, like the Eumenides, pursues you with rods of snakes" ("lecz ciebie przepędzi ma dusza,/ Jak Eumenida, przez wężowe rózgi"). In Aeschylus' *Oresteia*, the Eumenides are portrayed as gorgons with snakes for hair.[1]

---

1 See *The Libation Bearers*: "they come like gorgons, they/wear robes of black, and they are wreathed in a tangle/ of snakes" (ll.1048–1050). The

(Słowacki's use of the Polish expression for the military punish-
ment "running the gauntlet" makes the image contemporary.[2]) In
the *Libation Bearers* (ll. 527, 531, 524), Aeschylus tells us that
Clytemnestra "dreamed she gave birth to a snake. . . . She her-
self, in the dream, gave her breast to suck." And just before she
is murdered by Orestes, her final words to him are: "You are the
snake I gave birth to, and gave breast" (l. 929). The imagery of
snakes here in reference to her death at her son's hands and the
double invocation of "curse" in this stanza and the next one,
which we will discuss below, point to Aeschylus as the literary
source of this part of Słowacki's poem.

The Prometheus myth is better known: the Titan who
rebelled against Zeus' rule became a popular emblem of protest
and sacrifice. In the legend he was chained to a rock by Zeus
for stealing fire to help mortals; his punishment was eternal
torment by an eagle that ate his liver every day. Each day the
liver grew back, thus evoking a view of unending torment. In
the Romantic period the eagle, a noble bird and the symbol of
Zeus himself, was transformed into the lowly vulture who
feeds on carrion, as in Shelley's *Prometheus Unbound* or
Byron's "Prometheus" ("The rock, the vulture, and the chain").

Słowacki may have borrowed the idea of a vulture from the
British poets, but he had his own reason to do so. He makes the
distinction that the vulture does not pick at Poland's heart (the

image is repeated in the first scene of *The Eumenides*. Trans. R.
Lattimore (Chicago: University of Chicago Press, 1953).

2   Juliusz Kleiner notes the phrase in his commentary to *Lilla Weneda i
Gròb Agamemnona* ([Warszawa: Nakład Gebethnera i Wolffa, 1923], p.
182). Running the gauntlet was still a common punishment in the
Russian army, and in Lev Tolstoy's *Hadji Murat* (1888) it is mentioned
in particular as a favorite punishment of Nicholas I against his Polish
subjects; one wonders if this would be the association in the minds of
Słowacki's audience as well. In any case, Słowacki has decided to adopt
the most severe punishment he could imagine against his own country.

seat of faith and passion) but at its brain (the seat of reason), thus forcing the reader to consider what exactly is being criticized here. It is not clear who the vulture is, but in *Beniowski* it is identified as Słowacki's critics from the journal *Młoda Polska* (the "friends" of Mickiewicz, also "imitators").[3] He writes here: "my brain was your food – but my heart stretches like a bow – it shakes you off, you generation of vultures" ("Z mòzgu mojego mieliście jedzenie, – lecz serce moje się jak łuk wypręża – zrzuca was głodne sępòw pokolenie"). In fact, in *Beniowski* Słowacki extends his criticism from these critics to the Polish nobility as a whole, and revives the imagery of *Agamemnon's Tomb*: he refers to the Poles as "knights without swords" (canto III, l. 535; cf. the "half-knights" in *Agamemnon's Tomb*). Most strikingly, he rejects "clothing" for a noble "nakedness": he declares that what Poland needs is a sculptor like Phidias, capable of producing a statue of Leonidas, rather than "tailors" (canto III, lines 537–539; cf. the "parrot and peacock of nations" in *Agamemnon's Tomb*).[4] What was more mildly expressed in *Agamemnon's Tomb* – probably because of Słowacki's deference to Czartoryski and the audience members, and his ambitions to be heard by them sympathetically – is unleashed in gleeful malice in *Beniowski*, when the poet has already been rejected by his readers. But the core of the argument is the same, and the same imagery from Antiquity is used to make his point in both works.

The final lines in stanza 20 (the stanza about Prometheus) mark a further switch from convention: the poet and his muse

3   *Beniowski*, in Słowacki, *Dzieła* [*Works*] , vol. 3, pp.76–77; *Poland's Angry Romantic. Two Poems and a Play by Juliusz Słowacki.* Edited and translated by Peter Cochran, Bill Johnston, Mirosława Modrzewska and Catherine O'Neil (Cambridge: Cambridge Scholars, 2009), p. 252. Cf. III [13], p. 235.
4   See also Sinko, *Hellenizm Juliusza Słowackiego*, pp. 114–115, on the connections between *Agamemnon's Tomb* and *Beniowski*.

become the vulture, tearing at the body to extract the "core." The word he uses here, "trzewia," evokes an image of the core of a tree, which is at odds with the original Prometheus myth and the role of the vulture.[5] Słowacki's Prometheus is very much a Christ figure, a savior who sacrificed himself for the sake of mankind. By naming Poland a modern-day Prometheus Słowacki suggests Poland has made a great sacrifice and is suffering as a result. In stanza 16 Słowacki presents Poland in a continuous state of suffering by being endlessly chopped to pieces (but not dying). Likewise the hyena, which alludes to the foreign powers that partitioned or dismembered Poland, endlessly prowls over the half-dead corpse of the nation. Finally, Słowacki suggests that Poland has not been properly buried; hence the image of open eyes. This state of perpetually renewing torment and a deathlike state in life reinforces the comparison of Poland to Prometheus.

However, Słowacki complicates any reading of Poland simply as either an innocent martyr or savior by referring to two faculties – brain and heart. Instead of emphasizing Poland's suffering he is pointing to what makes her weak: it is the brain that is at fault.[6] Moreover, unlike Heracles' shirt, the Polish version of Deianira's shirt is not an enemy's trick; it is

5   As we mentioned earlier (see p. 39) the image of shaking the tree and the blood comes, perhaps, from the story of Polydorus in Virgil. In this passage Aeneas says: "Soon as I tear the first stalk/from its roots and rip it up from the earth . . ./dark blood oozes out and fouls the soil with filth./Icy shudders rack my limbs – my blood chills with fear./But again I try, I tear at another stubborn stalk – /I'll probe this mystery to its hidden roots." (III, ll. 34–39, Robert Fagles, trans.). The similarity is only in form, not in content. In Virgil, the surprised Aeneas shakes the tree to find out why blood is oozing out; in Słowacki, shaking has the character of vengeance, as if the poet were trying to awaken Poland and bring back the rational faculty.
6   Cf. *Beniowski*, III [13], in *Poland's Angry Romantic*, p. 235.

self-imposed. The dismemberment of Poland's "body" and the preying of foreign "hyenas" is a consequence of the lack of reason, faulty judgment and misguided politics that led to Poland's death. This stanza struck Józef Tretiak for reasons that are difficult to immediately understand when the poem is read in English, a language without gender. The word "Poland" (Polska) in Polish is feminine, whereas Prometheus is masculine. However, what for the Polish scholar was a jarring dissonance, is also striking in any language for contextual reasons. It is rather surprising to find the figure of Prometheus which appears like a *deus ex machina*; there is no connection between the ancient *Oresteia* and Prometheus, with the exception, perhaps, of the fact that it is Heracles who frees Prometheus from the rock. Yet the thematic link seems to be weak and it is difficult to see how it might help to advance the interpretation of the poem.

Part 8.
A Note on Słowacki's Messianism.

A link between Heracles' apotheosis and Prometheus and their association with the nation of Poland can be established through Messianism. In its most general form, Messianism is a promise of the regeneration of mankind by Christ the Messiah. In his *Books of the Polish Nation and the Polish Pilgrims*, Mickiewicz famously announced that Poland is the Christ of Nations. Poland, like the Messiah, suffered and was crucified, but its sacrifice was not in vain. Accordingly, the nation assumes the role of the savior of other nations, and it is endowed with its mission by history itself.

Mickiewicz's Messianism was often a source of mild "embarrassment" for scholars of Polish literature,[1] but it must be remembered that Messianism is not just a Polish phenomenon.[2]

---

1   See Czesław Miłosz, *The Land of Ulro*, trans. Louis Iribarne (New York: Farrar, Strauss Giroux, 1984), pp. 100–101.

2   In the French paper *Le Globe*, 29 January, 1832, for example, one can read: "La France a bu le calice revolutionnaire . . . la France a monté sur la croix. La France a été le Christ de nations" Quoted in Andrzej Walicki, *Philosophy and Romantic Nationalism. The Case of Poland* (The University of Notre Dame Press: Notre Dame, 1994), p. 245. In his very erudite and well documented work, Walicki discusses the inspira-

Nonetheless, the motif of Messianism has particular significance in Polish Romanticism. A people who had lost their country had to find some kind of consolation, and they did this by seeing its political martyrdom as having a greater goal. Accordingly, they developed a messianic doctrine whereby Poland died as a country only to rise, just like Christ, in full glory.

If Messianism is instinctively associated with Mickiewicz's name, Słowacki is seldom seen as a poet who expounds a messianic vision of Poland as the redeemer of nations and the herald of a new political order.[3] He never wrote his own version of the *Book of the Polish Pilgrims*, nonetheless his remarks scattered in his letters and unfinished fragments contain ample evidence of an aggressive Messianism in his thought. It is enough to quote from one of these: "But we await the resurrection of old Poland from the Divine spirit as the Messiah of Nations, which will be born neither from earth nor clouds, but from our hearts and our spirits, and will appear as the Savior of millions. . . . ."[4]

tional sources of Polish Messianism. The book also includes chapters on Mickiewicz and Słowacki. However, one needs to point out that they do not seem to be of equal value. The chapter dedicated to Mickiewicz gives a much more thorough account than the one on Słowacki.

3   Under the influence of Towiański, a religiously inspired charlatan, Mickiewicz stopped writing and became more and more religiously inspired. (For a comparative discussion of Mickiewicz's Messianism, see Manfred Kridl, "Two Champions of a New Christianity: Lamennais and Mickiewicz," *Comparative Literature*, Vol. 4, No. 3 (Summer, 1952): pp. 239–267.)

Słowacki underwent a so-called "mystical" period. A sober analysis of his writings shows that his language is not reminiscent of the language of religious mystics. Even if we make the disclaimer that the writings of poets do not lend themselves to the same kind of scrutiny as those of philosophers or politicians, Słowacki's late writings, where the poet expresses himself on political themes, particularly with reference to Homer as a teacher of politics, make very little sense and do not amount to coherent theory.

4   *Dzieła [Works]*, vol. XII, p. 238–239.

This is not the place to reconstruct Słowacki's theory of Messianism,[5] but rather to point out what others have seemingly overlooked, namely, its Greekness.

Agamemnon's Tomb is never mentioned as the place where Słowacki formulated any messianic ideas, despite the fact that in more than one way Messianism is central to its ideological underpinning, as the theme of the grave leads to the idea of resurrection and salvation. What is striking about the way the theme is worked out in the poem is that he picks the least obvious image of resurrection and salvation: Prometheus.

There were three symbols of resurrection common in art in this period in particular: the Phoenix, Christ, and Prometheus. If Słowacki's ultimate goal in *Agamemnon's Tomb* was to criticize his nation with an eye to its betterment and with Poland's return to the map of Europe, the image of the Phoenix in the stanza analyzed in the last section would have done equally well. As a matter of fact, for purely imaginative purposes the Phoenix rising from the ashes should have been very appealing: it would have shown the indestructibility of a Poland that springs up after being annihilated.[6] As we have mentioned, the second image of resurrection, Christ, and Poland as the Christ of nations, was already popular from the works of Mickiewicz and others. The least fitting, perhaps, of all savior models was Prometheus. It is tempting to regard the explanation for this choice of Prometheus as because of all three symbols, only Prometheus is a Greek. Bringing in Christ or the Phoenix would mean incorporating symbols from traditions alien to the

---

5   Andrzej Walicki tries to grapple with Słowacki's Messianism in *Philosophy and Romantic Nationalism*, pp. 277–291.

6   The image of the Phoenix was used often in another messianic tradition: that of Russian Romanticism. The burning of Moscow during the Napoleonic wars invited frequent evocations of this image – Russia will rise again, Moscow will retain its primacy as Third (and final) Rome.

motifs of *Agamemnon's Tomb*. (With the exception of the harp, the druidic stones, the oak tree and the "North," there are virtually no non-Greek elements in the poem, and even these are incorporated with great subtlety.) One should note, however, that Słowacki's Prometheus is not an entirely original Greek figure either. He is not a rebellious Titan who, besides bringing aid and creative fire to humanity, wants to rival the father of the gods. The line where Prometheus appears and the words attached to him ("For you are Prometheus's only son") establishes his fatherhood, which we do not find in any original Greek account.

The range of interpretive venues is wide here, and the persona of Prometheus in the Romantic period had several variants, each of which suits the need of the individual poet. In Goethe's poem, Prometheus is like the Biblical God who lowers himself by empathizing with the human lot:

Here I sit, fashion humans
In my own image,
A breed to be my equal,
To suffer, sorrow,
To enjoy and be joyful,
And to ignore you,
Like me. ("Prometheus," 1774)[7]

In Byron, Prometheus is a symbol of man and his condition, very much like man from the great Renaissance humanist, Pico della Mirandola:

A mighty lesson we inherit:
Thou art a symbol and a sign

---

7   Goethe, *Selected Poems*, trans. John Whaley (London: J. M. Dent, 1998), p. 21.

To Mortals of their fate and force;
Like thee, Man is in part divine, (1816)[8]

Shelley's Prometheus is a complex study of the perfectibility of mankind, the Titan-son born of a tyrant-father (Jove), a better son than his father. Słowacki does not seem to endow Prometheus with any of the qualities we find in the German or British poets. In Słowacki, Prometheus is the father and Poland is the son. The son's mission is to continue his father's work, to suffer for the sake of man, to be mankind's benefactor. Endowing Poland (a feminine noun) with sonhood, which struck Tretiak as a dissonance inconsistent with the gender-laden Polish, was intended by Słowacki, but was at the same time impossible to resolve. The simple grammatical solution to avoid the gender clash between the feminine Poland and the masculine son would be to say: "because you are Prometheus' only daughter." However, the use of "daughter" would deprive the poem of the most immediate association of Poland as Christ – the son of God – who made the sacrifice. By creating the gender dissonance, Słowacki ingeniously shifted emphasis, and the reader's attention, almost as if knocking on the door of his cultural subconscious, from the childless Greek Prometheus to the Biblical God and his Son.

The messianic conception of a nation creates several problems. One of them is the analogy between the death of the Messiah and his miraculous resurrection on the one hand and the death of a collective, and consequently, the possibility of its resurrection on the other hand, and its mission as a savior of other nations. This difficulty was apparent to Słowacki in a poem composed during his voyage to the Holy Land,

---

8   Byron, *Complete Poetical Works*, ed. Frederick Page, rev. John Jump (Oxford: Oxford University Press, 1970), p. 98.

"Conversation with the Pyramids." Let us quote the last two
stanzas:

O pyramids, do you have inside
Such coffins and sarcophagi,
To lay the naked sword thereby,
Our vengeance in this blade to hide,
Bury, and embalm with fragrance,
And for the future keep safe perchance?
Come in through our gates with this sword,
We have such coffins in our ward.

O pyramids – do you have inside
Such coffins and such sepulchers,
Where our martyrs could be laid for years
In balsamed garments side by side;
So that each one on the glory day
Returned to his land whole, though as clay?
–Give us those people without a stain,
We have such coffins in our domain.[9]

The last of these stanzas states that a nation can be pre-
served for the day of resurrection; the final stanza unambigu-
ously implies that the sacrifice must be made from the poet's
own spirit so that the nation can be called back to life. If so,
strange as it sounds, Słowacki himself assumes the role of the
Messiah. This "incarnation" is not as bizarre as it sounds. First,
it is consistent with a similar "trick" in *Agamemnon's Tomb*,
when the poet is both Orestes and the Eumenides. In fact, the
role of "castigator" of his people is in the Biblical prophetic

9   Translated by Michael J. Mikos in Juliusz Słowacki, *This Fateful Power.
    Sesquicentennial Anthology 1809–1849* (Lublin, Norbertinum, 1999),
    pp. 49–51.

tradition more than in the Greek – the Eumenides punish individual crimes, not the wrongs of a whole nation – and thus is fitting with messianic art.[10] Professing oneself as Christ may sound blasphemous, but Słowacki seems to have a point. The poet wants to bury his spirit in a coffin, something that the pyramids do not have for the reason that spirit cannot be buried in a coffin. It is possible that in writing those lines Słowacki had in mind the evangelical story of the women who on the third day after Jesus' burial came to the physical tomb and were told not to look for the living among the dead.

Within a poetical world conceived like this, poetry assumes a power that makes and saves nations, and the poet becomes the Messiah.

It is only proper here to quote a few stanzas from another major poem by Słowacki, "My Testament," to illustrate how Słowacki saw his own role as a poet:

I have lived with you, suffered and shed tears with you.
No noble person have I ever passed aside.
Today I leave you, ghosts in shadows to pursue,
And if happiness were here – in sorrow I stride.

I have not left behind me a single offspring
Either to play my lute or to carry my name;
My name has passed away like a flash of lightning,
And will last for generations like an empty strain.

But you that have known me, pass to all the legend
That I wore out my youth for the land of my fathers;

---

10   Janion and Żmigrodzka write about Słowacki's later mystical period, in discussing the poem "Narody lecz": "In his mystical period Słowacki was no longer the tormented blasphemer but a punishing prophet, the apocalyptic avenger of the people's wrongs" (*Romantyzm i historia*, p. 71).

When the ship struggled – I stood at the mast to the end,
And when she was sinking – I too drowned in deep
waters . . .

[. . .]

As for me – I am leaving a small group of friends,
Those who were able to love my haughty spirit;
One can see I have fulfilled God's hard assignments
And assented to have here – an unwept casket . . .

[. . .]

And yet I leave behind me this fateful power,
Useless while I live . . . it just graces my temples;
But when I die, it will, unseen, press you ever,
Till it remakes you, bread eaters – into angels.[11]

The idea in the last line is elaborated elsewhere:

And you, Helion [a fictitious Greek character], you will
see the heights of our spirits if you consider the national
character, its lack of concern for earthly things, those
inborn qualities which are recollection of and formation
of spirits acquired before birth.[12]

There are two points that need to be made here: first, the
idea of the formation of spirits and recollection and, second,
the lack of concern for earthly things that the spirits manifest.

11 Mikos, trans., *This Fateful Power*, pp. 29–31.
12 The idea of the recollection and preexistence of the souls comes from
    Plato's *Republic*, X, 614–521d ("The Myth of Er"), where Plato explains
    how souls join bodies.

The first takes us to Plato, particularly the end of the last Book of the *Republic*, where Plato explains how souls (spirits) pre-exist before their union with bodies. Plato's thought is like crutches on which Słowacki is trying to make his Messianism walk. If a soul can exist without a body, then nations can exist without a country. In a number of passages Słowacki suggests that the ideas of nations, just like ideas of men, pre-exist. In a short note titled "Ideas of Nations" Słowacki writes: "The Greek and Persian ideas fought a battle in the air, like two angels; Marathon, Thermopylae and Platea were visible signs of [this battle] and proved that the numerical world is oftentimes in reverse relationship to the forces which fight over the world in the land of spirit."[13] Słowacki sees the physical world as the manifestation of invisible forces, spirits. (The primacy of Spirit will become characteristic of his whole later literary output.) From his scattered remarks, where constant references to Greece verge on the brink of obsession, the victory of the Greeks over the Persians is the victory of good over evil. The soul of a nation, in so far as it is different from other souls, must have been shaped prior to any possible union with its body. "Similarly, just as before the creation of the world there was the Word, that is a spirit that was supposed to reveal itself through visible forms, so the conception of each nation has been preceded by the creation of an idea, in which people, proper to this form, were crystallized."[14]

Secondly, a nation as spirit does not require ordinary earthly sustenance; so the individuals who are part of it must be different from others: they naturally manifest lack of concern for "ordinary bread." Nowhere is Słowacki's exaltation of Polishness more strongly expressed than in his letters to Prince

13 *Dzieła* [*Works*], vol. XII, p. 253.
14 *Dzieła* [*Works*], vol. XII, p. 253.

Adam Czartoryski, where he contrasts the French[15] and the Poles. "The French preoccupation: the continual pursuit of lowly laws of progress, for us it can be a trifle [*igraszka*] but not an ideal for the future, not a form, not a hope for a spirit like Yours [your Highness], forged . . . a hundred years old, like an oak."[16] And in a letter to George Sand he states: "It turns out that the French, who consider themselves Christian, so far have worked on behalf of paganism."[17] What was initially a theoretical construct, whose goal was to conceive a theory of nationality that would explain how a people without a country can exist, eventually assumed the form of criticism of contemporary Western political institutions and modern commercial society.[18]

As Andrzej Waśko notes, in Słowacki's later period, the period of the above quoted remarks, he moved from his original criticism in *Agamemnon's Tomb* and returned to the rehabilitation of the old Polish institutions, including the Golden Liberty. In support of Waśko's claim we can quote Słowacki's letter to George Sand:

> We were heralds of the freedom of individual conscience, our fathers felt sufficient power to create a new human form according to Divine laws. They failed and suffered

15 Słowacki's anti-French obsession is well known. See, for example, *Dzieła* [*Works*], vol. XII, pp. 25–26, August 6, 1831, where he writes to his mother: "The English . . . London, delightful – Paris cannot stand comparison with it." He repeats this idea in his very next letter to his mother, after returning to Paris (letter of September 10, 1831) and writes negatively about French literature.

16 *Dzieła* [*Works*], vol. XII, p. 301.

17 In his second letter to Prince Adam Czartoryski Słowacki says that Homer and Hesiod would "bore their readers, like today's philosophers who consider constitutional government the ultimate [political] form." *Dzieła* [*Works*], vol. XIV, p. 367.

18 *Dzieła* [*Works*], vol. XII, p. 309.

not because they were too small or wretched but because they could not measure up to the demands of their own spirit. Not being able to achieve this perfect consensus through love, they craved to reach it in desperation through human means – they used that [liberum] veto like angels used the heavenly fire; to their own perdition. All we want is to rise in spirit so that we can begin the work of ideas where our forefathers left.[19]

Słowacki's rehabilitation reveals, however, a failure in his later position.[20] First, if the new generation, regenerated in the "Stygian mud" and unconcerned with earthly things, is destined to achieve what the old one failed to establish, Słowacki's messianic project comes down to nothing more than an "improved" version of the old institutions without any guarantee that they would work. Why did Słowacki rehabilitate the tradition he condemned in his poem? It is only a guess but this seems to explain the change in his position: once he accepted the thesis that national souls are pure before they join a body, the real nations or incarnations and their motivations must have appeared low and unclean, like the French in pursuit of lowly gains, and the realm of real politics fell short of the ideal.

How Słowacki imagined the transition from the realm of ideas (the spiritual republic) to the earthly realm remains unexplained. Depending on one's point of view, one can see in Słowacki's position an act of the poet's helplessness and

---

19 *Dzieła* [*Works*], vol. XIV, p. 369. Walicki writes that in this period (the period of *Król Duch*) Słowacki saw the *liberum veto* as "a precious device, by means of which the true spiritual hierarchy was able to defend itself against the false, artificial, material hierarchy" (*National and Religious Messianism*, p. 282).

20 *Romantyczny sarmatyzm*, p. 26.

desperation,[21] a lack of understanding of Western European politics,[22] or, which is more likely, just a failure on his part to create a viable political alternative to what he condemned in contemporary bourgeois Europe.

21 Compare the above with: "Having made this nation a wonder of the world, which, deprived of its fatherland, went to heaven to receive life – and received Divine fatherhood from God's hand over other nations." *Dzieła [Works]*, vol. XII, pp. 262–263.

22 "I believe, however, that the principle of all politics is unknown to anyone today, the science of knowing the spirits that Saint Paul mentions, which he counts among one of the sciences that we receive from the Holy Spirit . . ." 2nd Letter to Czartoryski, *Dzieła [Works]*, vol. XII, p. 313. Remarks like this are not uncommon in his late writings, be they poetic works or miscellaneous pieces such as letters.

Part 9.

Greek Connections: "Put a curse on your son and howl in pain."

The Prometheus image is immediately followed in the next two stanzas by a complex analogy surrounding Orestes and the Eumenides. There is a dramatic acceleration between the two stanzas, 21 and 22. In the first of these, Poland is a maid or servant; here she is a (female) slave. This acceleration is additionally intensified by the violence of the image of the poet's shaking to the very core of Poland's being, blood, and the introduction of the Eumenides or Furies.

[21]
Put a curse on your son and howl in pain,
But be aware – the cursing hand
You stretch over me – will coil like a serpent
And snap off, withered, from your shoulder,
And then black devils will snatch it up from the dust;
For you have no power to curse – you slave!

[22]
No, until with trembling hand

You cover your bare, widow's breast
I will not bend, even before a kneeling woman,
For I have another, sorrowful mother – glory –
Who dries my tears that seldom flow,
And I also have a third one I call mother . . .

There is a sudden change of subject matter in these stanzas. Słowacki moves from being the Eumenides to being the son, an unforgiving son, who refuses to lower himself and kneel before his supplicating mother despite the fact that she is placing her hands on her widowed breasts, as if she wanted to say: "can't you see that I suffer too." The poet's unfilial attitude verges on inhumanity and violates the biblical commandment to honor one's parents. Is there justification for the poet's attitude toward his widowed mother?

Once again, Słowacki is steeped here in the tradition of Greek Antiquity, where we find a precedent for such cruel words from a son to a mother. The poet's words lead us to Euripides and Aeschylus. Euripides in his *Orestes* says: "when from his mother's robes of golden weave he saw the breast rise to his gaze, he slaughtered his mother, making requital for his father's woes" (ll.837–843).[1] And: "If women are going to be brazen enough to kill their husbands, taking refuge with their children, appealing for pity by showing their breasts, it would be a trifle for them to kill their husbands for any grievance whatever" (ll. 569–565).

"Curse me..." in stanza 20, and "Put a curse on your son and howl in pain" in stanza 21, are reminiscent of Aeschylus's final exchange of words between Orestes and his mother Clytemnestra before he kills her in *The Libation Bearers* (ll. 924; 928). There Clytemnestra says: "Take care. Your mother's curse, like dogs, will drag you down. . . . You are the snake I

---

1   David Kovacs, trans., Loeb Classical Library (Cambridge, MA: Harvard University Press, 2002).

gave birth to, and gave the breast."[2] Słowacki's "[Then] curse me" sounds like a direct response to Clytemnestra's lines in the play. There is enough evidence to support Miłosz's claim about Słowacki's aggressiveness toward his country, and stanzas 20, 21 and 22 are indeed proverbial. However, here Słowacki's alleged aggression is not an expression of his personal feelings but a poetically stylized imitation of the material provided by ancient tragedians.[3] The gentle tone of stanza 24, that begins with "O, my poorest mother!" (an unlikely expression of mourning for the same mother whom Orestes mercilessly slaughtered for her transgression in all three playwrights), signals a departure from Greek dramatic violence.

Stanzas 20 to 23 are built on the imagery and themes of the Greek *Oresteia* trilogy, invoked at the very beginning of *Agamamnon's Tomb*, where we find the familiar figures of Electra, Orestes, and the Eumenides. The only persona that is absent by name and who plays a paramount role in the *Oresteia* is the god Apollo – the same god who incited Orestes to commit matricide and who is instrumental in saving him from the Eumenides. However, Apollo does appear later, in stanza 29, as the only god besides Jove who is invoked as Słowacki's poetic patron. One can also speculate that the beam of light entering Agamemnon's tomb at the beginning of the poem is Apollo, the Sun god.

Słowacki assumes two contrasting roles – the bloodstained matricide and the enraged agents of revenge, the Eumenides, in an earlier poem, entitled "My Nation" (Narodzie mòj):

---

2   *The Libation Bearers*, tr. by Richmond Lattimore, in Aeschylus – I (Chicago & London: The University of Chicago Press, 1953)

3   In the context of the play *Kordian*, drawing attention to Kordian's dying words, T. Sinko points out that "without Aeschylus's influence it would be difficult to explain those cosmic sympathies or defiant words uttered by Kordian as he awaits death." Sinko, *Hellenizm Juliusza Słowackiego*, p. 70.

Narodzie Mój,
Coś widział miecz
Na niebie ciemnym świecący,

Powròcę ja –
Patrz, Furia zła,
Przyjdę jak płomien gorący.[4]

[My nation, that has seen a sword gleaming in the sky
above, I will return – look, angry Fury, I will come like a
burning flame.]

Recall that in the last line of the previous stanza, before the
introduction of the Eumenides, Słowacki says "I am full of
guilt," as if in anticipation of the punishment of Słowacki as
Orestes the matricide and the introduction of Słowacki as
Orestes the avenger, who in turn must be punished by the
Eumenides.

In the stanza that immediately follows, elaborating on this
"third one whom he can call mother," Słowacki strikes a tone
of pity and love:

[23]
O, my poorest mother! I would like to send you
From the fields of Mycenae an urn filled with my ashes . . .
Throw two wedding rings into these ashes,
Beseech Diana and her gloomy spirits
To allow you to see me one more time
In the moonbeams . . . for I was cherished by you.

The stanza incorporates imagery not only from Antiquity
but also from Slavic culture. It marks a turn toward the Polish

---

4   Słowacki, *Dzieła* [*Works*], vol. I, p. 185.

thematic layer and an address to his real, biological mother in Poland. Yet it is a complex series of associations: the urn he mentions may be an allusion to the urn Electra unknowingly takes to be full of Orestes' ashes in Sophocles' *Electra* (ll. 1113–1159). In these lines Electra emphasizes her rightful place as a mother figure to her brother Orestes – and this makes the analogy in Słowacki's lines more plausible; his own mother would receive such an urn and weep that her son died in a foreign land. The opening stanzas of *Agamemnon's Tomb* which invoke Electra's meeting with what she thinks are her brother's ashes in Aeschylus' tragedy, is recalled in this passage.[5] The "motherly" relationship of Electra to Orestes is also suggested in Euripides' *Orestes* (ll. 221–222), where Electra says: "Such a menial task is a pleasure, and I do not refuse to tend my brother's body with sisterly touch."[6] Although she says "sisterly," she cares for him like his mother.

This reading of Słowacki's Electra as a mother figure is reinforced by the reference to Diana in this stanza, where he sends his mother an urn with his ashes and asks her to invoke his spirit by the moon goddess (Diana), by throwing in two wedding rings. Diana is invoked with wedding rings possibly because of her rejection of marriage: the son dies in a foreign land unmarried; the mother receives the symbol of his destiny. Diana's rejection of love is alluded to numerous times in Ovid's *Metamorphoses*, as are many other heroines who emulated her in escaping marriage: for example, Daphne, who "fled the very name of love, rejoicing in the deep fastnesses of the woods . . . vying with virgin Phoebe [Artemis/Diana]" (Bk. I, ll. 474–476).[7] Electra too is someone who eschewed

---

5   In the Aeschylus play, Orestes calls her "O, my poor one"; cf. Słowacki, "O najbiedniejsza!" ("Oh, my poor one") in stanza 23.

6   David Kovacs, trans.

7   Frank Justus Miller, trans., Loeb Classical Library (Cambridge, MA: Harvard UP, 1977).

marriage but (in Euripides) raised and cared for her brother as if he were her own son.[8] When one steps away from antiquity and examines the motif of the wedding rings, Diana (the moon), and the conjuring of a vision of a beloved man, the motif seems to draw upon fortune-telling in Slavic folklore.[9] In this mythological trope the woman calls up a vision of her bridegroom by moonlight with the help of mirrors or candle-wax. Given the specificity of the allusion to Słowacki's real mother, the wedding/bridegroom imagery is strange – but also understandable.

In fact, Słowacki seems to associate Electra with his real mother, as several other references attest. For example, in *Beniowski* a cancelled stanza contains one of Słowacki's most beautiful apostrophes to his mother: "Above Electra's stream you were with me./ In every place where a voice of lament carries from the past, o my dear one/[. . .] everywhere where an envious man – is dead and the desire for death drinks the soul – You were with me." To Krasiński he wrote: "You, whom we saw in the dark tomb of Agamemnon; you who once rode along the banks of the laurel stream where the Princess Electra starched the mother's shroud."[10] Thus the role of Electra as a mother figure and as a link with his own mother in his days in

8   Euripides' Electra says: "Dearest brother, how you cheered me when you fell asleep! Shall my hands soothe your distress?" and: "There! Such a menial task is a pleasure, and I do not refuse to tend my brother's body with sisterly touch" (ll. 217–218, 221–222). Euripides, *Orestes*, David Kovacs trans.

9   The motif is well-captured in Russian romantic poetry, from Zhukovsky's ballad *Svetlana* to Pushkin's Tatiana in *Eugene Onegin*. However, it is also found in other national traditions: for example the German ballad *Lenore* by Burger, on which these Slavic variants are drawn (as well as, for example, Keats' "The Eve of St. Agnes").

10   The phrase is "bieli płòtno" – the same words we find in stanza 2 of *Agamemnon's Tomb*. Quoted in Sinko, Hellenizm *Juliusza Słowackiego*, pp. 111–112.

exile is made expressly by Słowacki at several points at the time (or around the time) the poem was composed. Electra is the very first of the Atreides mentioned by Słowacki in the poem – it is her voice that answers his in the gloom – and Sophocles' tragedy focuses on the idea of burial: who may be buried, who has the right to mourn, etc. Thus the "house of crime" Słowacki mentions in stanza 1 seems to recall the full circle of violence. Orestes is "resurrected" after this scene – he proves to his sister he is indeed alive and goes on to murder Clytemnestra.

[24]
Now I am nothing – but these ghosts
That surround me . . . swirl about
And point to the garlands and speak the cant
Of angelic spirits . . . I will go . . . my blood is burning;
Already judged, I sing like a swan,
But when my song comes to you, what will happen to you!

This torment resembles that of Orestes in Euripides' tragedy, when he "burns" in torment of his "judgment" and sees the Eumenides as terrifying visions.[11] First he sees the vengeance of his mother: "Mother, I beg you, don't loose on me those bloody-faced, snaky maidens" (ll. 255–256).

[25]
You laughed – it seems like yesterday –
When you found me sad one time
And weeping over Hector's death.
These were not foolish tears, nor were they childish.

---

11 Chorus: "What malady, what tears, what pitiful fate is greater in the world than to take a mother's blood upon one's hands? From doing such deed he has been driven wild with fits of madness, the Eumenides' quarry, his darting eyes rolling in fear, he, Agamemnon's son." Euripides, *Orestes*, ll. 830–835.

My tears are more foolish now . . . and flow more often,
When I recall my fate – ah, my tears are a hundred times
more bitter.

In another letter to his mother Słowacki writes: "Do you
know that I myself sat alone for an entire hour in
Agamemnon's tomb and thought about my metal armor, shed-
ding tears, while the crickets filled the grave with their words,
like a nymph of the past commanding silence."[12] Again, the
poem contains fragments of his experience in his travels.
In stanza 22 the poet moves from Greek themes to the
motif of his mother. Scholars have long noted Słowacki's
obsessive love for his mother,[13] Salomea Becu, but the change
in tone is surprising in such a mytho-historical poem. However,
when we consider the theme of mothers and the theme of
"crime against mothers" the various threads of the poem come
together. Orestes may have had to avenge the death of his
father, but the Eumenides must punish him for killing his
mother.[14]

12 Allusion suggested by Sinko, *Hellada i Roma w Polsce, ibid.*, p. 115.
13 For example, in his letter or 16 February 1841 (Mikos, *This Fateful
    Power*, p. 137), Słowacki writes to his mother: "I have never thought,
    dear, that you stopped loving me. Alas! Nobody in the world can love as
    much as you – it only pains me that I cannot prove my love for you at
    all . . ."
14 Chorus: "Whoso holdeth out hands undefiled, no wrath from us assaileth
    him, and unscathed he passeth all his days; but whoso committeth sin as
    this man hath, and hideth his blood-stained hands, as upright witness for
    the slain do we present ourselves, and as avengers of bloodshed do we
    appear against him to the end." Aeschylus, *Eumenides* (ll. 310–320),
    translated by Herbert Weir Smyth, Loeb Classical Library (Cambridge,
    MA: Harvard UP, 1972). And in Ian Johnston's translation they say:
    "That man killed his mother – he must pay!" (line 311);" I'll drag you
    down, [. . .] and there you'll pay for murdering your mother."

Part 10.

Conclusion.

If the tragedies of Aeschylus, Sophocles and Euripides present the Greek story, Słowacki presents his own dramatized version of the history of Poland in the form of a poem. The poet assumes the role of Orestes, to whom Electra speaks at the beginning of the poem from a laurel leaf. Like Orestes, who comes to avenge the death of their father, Słowacki comes to avenge the death of his fatherland.

[26]
O cranes, forming your ranks toward the north
Above the mountain of Corinth,
Bear on your wings my gloomy song,
Carry it with you . . . maybe some night in the future
This hollow song will fly over my land
Like a bell lamenting in the world of the spirit.

[27]
O cranes! You, who in the rose-colored sky
Will rise in the morning like a trailing scarf,
You were once beloved of me,
You were my autumn harp!

You – and the pine trees rustling above the graves,
Where can I see you today?

[28]
And yet . . . I sensed even in the spring of life
That I would be unhappy one day and guilty . . .
That perhaps misfortune would grow from my heart
And I would not have the first crown among spirits,
And that one day, wild with sorrow,
I would leave you – engulfed in golden dawn.

The motif of the cranes (and birds in general) signifies
wandering and homelessness. Władysław Folkierski traces the
motif to one of Słowacki's major sources in the *Voyage*:
Chateaubriand, who in his *Itineraire* wrote of the storks that fly
to Africa every year and return to find what they knew before
in ruins.[1] Cranes have a particular meaning for the "northern"
tribes, Poles and Russians, for whom they are harbingers of
spring and hope. In Mickiewicz's first Crimean Sonnet,
"Akkerman Steppes," the cranes suggest the motherland, a
return to home for the exiled poet: "I hear cranes too high up
for a falcon's eyes [. . .] one could almost make out/ A call from
Lithuania." Słowacki invokes them in the same way here.

[29]
Today your hour has come . . . be well!
There the gleaming archipelago calls me,
There Corinth keeps its crowned head,

---

1 Władysław Folkierski, *Od Chateaubrianda do Anhellego. Rzecz o
   związkach między przedmistycznym okresem Słowackiego a roman-
   tyzmem francuskim* [From Chateaubriand to Anhelli. On the
   Relationship Between the pre-Mystical period in Słowacki and French
   Romanticism] (Kraków: Polska Akademja Umiejętności/Gebethner i
   Wolff, 1924), pp. 63–72.

And beyond the Lepanto ancient Parnassus rises . . .
O my muse! How should you greet
The mountain where Apollo and Zeus have sat?

[30]
O Romantic muse, on your knees!
For I will bow to this mountain
From the fragrant linden tree of classical Jan,
And from the singer of children and monks
and from the singer of the Potockis' garden,
And I will send a quiet, tearful bow . . . from my father.

[31]
I know that now he is here with me in spirit,
Although harsh death has closed his eyes;
And the rustling of this fig tree
In my ear is like – the whisper of lips . . .
I hear . . . although I can no longer recall my father's voice
This must be his voice – for it is sorrowful.

[32]
For sometimes death calls us even after death
In a sad and not quite audible voice.
O mountain, shining in the light of the red moon
Like a bloody volcano . . . o, break into bits . . .
For you are mocked by the sparrows' chirping
And early crowing of the morning cock.
. . .

The last four stanzas culminate in a rejection of Romanticism
ostensibly in favor of Classicism.[2] In the invocation of stanza 30

2   See Jarosław Maciejewski's very informative article "Słowacki – prze-
     ciwnik romantyków" ("Słowacki –A Foe of the Romantics") *Studia*

the poet commands his Romantic muse to her knees before the classical Parnassus ("where Apollo and Jove have sat"), forcing her to an attitude of humility. The subsequent list of supplicants to the mountain consists of references to Polish Classicism and its homey thematics: Kochanowski's linden tree, and his poetry of sorrow for his daughter's death, and finally, the poet's own father, the classical scholar. From stanza 31 to the beginning of 32 Słowacki develops the theme of his father and returns to imagery he used at the beginning of the poem: the voice from the grave combined with the natural world, some contact with the past and the dead. In this way the tone returns to the elegiac opening of the poem. Then, in the final stanza, he addresses the mountain and employs violent, startling imagery of high Romanticism (or even the sublime).

In his address to the mountain Słowacki uses the paradoxical image of a "red moon" that makes the mountain look like a "bloody volcano." Elsewhere in the poem the moon is silvery; the mountain "classical." Here a violent and unnatural image is drawn. The trope of the volcano would most likely call to the mind of Słowacki's readers the famous lines by Mickiewicz, who wrote in *Dziady*: "Our people are like lava,/ On the surface cold and ugly,/ But a hundred years of internal fire will not be extinguished/ Let us spit on this shell and step into the depths." If the juxtaposition of Mickiewicz's lava with a bloody Romantic volcano that colors the moon red can be made, its redness must be read against the blood that resulted from the Uprising, spilt in response to Mickiewicz's call to action. According to Jarosław Maciejewski, this is consistent with the "anti-Romantic" stance Słowacki exhibits throughout his work: "The tragic youth who followed

Polonistyczne, V, 1977 (Poznań, 1978): pp. 67–80; cf. also, Maria Kalinowska, "Słowackiego Greckie Sny o Polsce." Cf. *Beniowski*, Canto I [25], in *Poland's Angry Romantic*, p. 177.

Romanticism, who – indecisive and immature, confused and alienated – led the whole nation to catastrophe, could be judged, naturally, in this very manner only after 1831: in *Lambro*, in *Kordian*, in *Piast Dantyszek*. [. . .] He considered himself back then and later to be a man susceptible to this all-powerful erroneous and harmful poetic fashion."[3] That call implies that Romanticism needs to ask forgiveness, to humble itself, for its immaturity led to the waste of the uprising. The ridiculing of the mountain by common birds – sparrows – is a sudden leap from the sublime to ordinary life. It is profoundly ambiguous: it suggests life goes on, and the upheavals of violence are made ridiculous. However, the crowing of cocks signals a call to awakening, a new day breaking. This is a call to release some vital force in Poland – Słowacki's image of a "bloody volcano" and a red moon on the most obvious level continues this image. Given this allusion to Mickiewicz – a serious and central trope of political significance in Romanticism – the roosters and sparrows with which Słowacki ends his poem are startlingly comic. The irreverence he uses to speak of his own poetry and inspiration begins earlier, with his allusions to Kochanowski and the other poets ("nightingales") of Poland, in stanza 30. The hominess of their subject matter, usually exalted as the strength of Polish literature, is seemingly dismissed by Słowacki. Polish local color is introduced in an ambiguous way.

It is worth comparing these lines with passages from Byron's *Childe Harold* I, stanzas 60–62, in which the poet describes his own encounter with Parnassus.

O, thou Parnassus! whom I now survey,
Not in the phrensy of a dreamer's eye,

---

3   Maciejewski, "Słowacki – przeciwnik romantyków," p. 71.

Not in the fabled landscape of a lay,
But soaring snow-clad through thy native sky,
In the wild pomp of mountain majesty!
What marvel if I thus essay to sing?
The humblest of thy pilgrims passing by
Would gladly woo thine Echoes with his string,
Though from thy heights no more one Muse will wave
her wing.

Oft have I dream'd of Thee! whose glorious name
Who knows not, knows not man's divinest lore;
And now I view thee, 'tis, alas! with shame
That I in feeblest accents must adore,
When I recount thy worshippers of yore
I tremble and can only bend the knee;
Nor raise my voice, nor vainly dare to soar,
But gaze beneath thy cloudy canopy
In silent joy to think at last I look on Thee!

Happier in this than mightiest bards have been,
Whose fate to distant homes confined their lot,
Shall I unmoved behold the hallow'd scene,
Which others rave of, though they know it not?
Though here no more Apollo haunts his grot,
And thou, the Muses' seat, art now their grave,
Some gentle spirit still pervades the spot,
Sighs in the gale, keeps silence in the cave,
And glides with glassy foot o'er yon melodious wave.

This unambiguous homage to Parnassus emphasizes at the
same time its importance (as the main inspiration for poetry)
and its weakness (the muses are dead, Apollo is gone).
Słowacki follows the passage by repeating some of Byron's
tropes – kneeling, silence, spirit – but disrupts the simple

homage. Like Byron, he also contrasts himself with his distant predecessors, in this case the poets of Poland. But where Byron seems to have in mind all his poetic predecessors, Słowacki displaces the significance of the contrast. He raises the ghost of his father, a "gentle spirit," as Byron says. Słowacki's father was a well known and an enthusiastic classicist, who died when the poet was five years old. The passage about Parnassus engages in the debate between Romanticism and Classicism. The authors of Classicism, who are represented by Parnassus, include Virgil, Homer, Dante and Shakespeare, and the Poles Kochanowski,[4] Krasicki[5] and Trembecki.[6] In Canto I of *Voyage to the Holy Land*, the poet describes his view of Naples from Virgil's grave, which seems to support Libera's reading. Kalinowska reads the transformation of Parnassus from "classical home of the muses" to "bloody volcano" and "red moon" as an admission that he can only operate in the realm of Romanticism.[7]

I part with you as well, O handful of dust,
Forever at rest under the classical laurel tree;
The rumble of carts and the Pauzi dungeons
Call in a romantic hymn beneath you.
That glory will pass, but the carts will not pass.
That cart road is an Aeneid of the centuries.

4   Kochanowski is the Renaissance "father of Polish poetry," one of whose major works is a poem on classical themes, *Dismissal of the Greek Messengers*.
5   Ignacy Krasicki (1735–1801), author of the mock-heroic poem *Monachomachia* (*War of the Monks*, 1778).
6   Stanisław Trembecki (1739–1812), author of "Sofiòwka" (1806), a panegyric poem centered around the garden of Zofia Potocka.
7   See Maria Kalinowska's discussion in "Greckie sny Słowackiego."

Compare this passage with Byron's comment on Greece and her ruins: "Art, Glory, Freedom fail, but Nature still is fair." (CHP II:87). Słowacki's lines at once evoke life and vibrancy, but deny that very life by reducing it to mere "carts" and the passage of glory.

Part 11.

Sunrise over Salamis:
The Sleeping Knights.

Although it was never published in Słowacki's lifetime, the extant final canto to *The Voyage*, the ninth, does provide an alternate conclusion to *Agamemnon's Tomb*, which immediately precedes it. The final stanzas of the canto comprise a rhapsody on Salamis, "Sunrise over Salamis." Like the cocks crowing at the end of Canto 8, the motif of "sunrise" seems to signal a call for a new dawn:

[20]
I call as my witnesses those last lines,
If they contain even a pennyworth of poetry
Don't be afraid, let your criticism pay the price –
I can take more from my enemies–
These lines are bad, so tell me so up front;
I wrote as if I'd never been in Sparta;

[21]
These lines are bad – here, I'll even grant it;
Unpoetic . . . I grant this too . . .

Come here to me . . . look . . . the shining water
Sports beneath my winged boat.
The boat breaks from the awakened wave
Like the most beautiful swan on Olympus.

[22]
The pale moon in the full sails
Shows me sailors lost in thought;
They stand like ancient knights of Hellas,
They lean on the mast . . . they have
Gilded spears and white cloaks . . .
The moon shines bright and gold upon them.

[23]
They know how to stay motionless
Like statues, looking at the clear sky;
Aeolus himself tames the furious winds,
And from their sails forms silvery shells,
In which they dwell, half-hidden,
Like spirits – freed by the thought of a bard.

[24]
It was quiet, and then suddenly – O blessed hour!
The boat pitched forward in the sea's depths
And with a groan suddenly shook . . .
This was the first wave of Salamis:
It ran up to meet its first Pole
And shook me hard . . . and groaned, and lay still.

[25]
And after it other waves ran up from the bank,
With a great roar, spreading with a sigh.
Dawn burst out with a vivid flame.

The sun shone . . . already bright from its ascent;
I thought that in this eternal land
It would rise in thunder – like God on Sinai.

In this final canto the poet is blessed by the sun deity, the pastoral scene and nature itself (the waves, wind and moon). The victorious Greeks, the spirits left at Salamis, come to life and the wave greets him ("the first Pole"), apparently acknowledging him as national poet.

Here Słowacki returns to the imagery of the denouement of *Agamemnon's Tomb* and Canto IV: the moon is silver and gold, reflecting the armor of the spirits. The Romantic image of poetry and inspiration (moon, wind, waves) are intact and unproblematic in this canto – unlike the "red moon" of *Agamemnon's Tomb*. The evocation of Salamis signals the Greek victory – against numerical odds, over the vast Persian army. It is the victors, the heroes of Salamis whom he not only addresses, but who also respond to his poetic call. The entire canto suggests Słowacki comes forth as champion of the national destiny.

The fact remains that, beautiful as the Salamis stanzas are, Słowacki did not attach them to *Grób Agamemnona* (or, for that matter, include them in *Beniowski*). Either the lofty and optimistic implications of this passage were too much at odds with his understanding of the contemporary Polish situation, or he could not quite cast himself so overtly in the role of poet-prophet (as the stanzas would require). We are left with his published diatribes, the poem that ends on the word "slave" and the satirical epic that derides everyone and everything in Poland.

Index of Proper Names
and Other Works by Słowacki